THE GARDEN LOVER'S GUIDE

SAN FRANCISCO BAY AREA

THE GARDEN LOVER'S GUIDE

Ron Sullivan

CHRONICLE BOOKS
SAN FRANCISCO

Printed in the United States of America.

Library of Congress Cataloging-in-Publication
Data available.
ISBN 0-8118-1877-2

Cover photography: Inset of leaves, Photonica, Katsumi Suzuki; inset: gloves,
courtesy of Smith & Hawken; photo of watering cans, Brenda Rae Eno
Design and illustrations: Brenda Rae Eno

Distributed in Canada by Raincoast Books,
8680 Cambie Street, Vancouver, B.C. V6P 6M9

10 9 8 7 6 5 4 3 2 1

Chronicle Books
85 Second Street
San Francisco, CA 94105

Web Site: www.chronbooks.com

For Joe

ACKNOWLEDGMENTS

Thanks to Chris Clarke, former editor of TERRAIN, who told me I ought to write about gardening; to Dennis Makishima, who sent me up a tree; to Denise Graham Lea and the rest of the Merritt College Hort Department and other friends who passed along great loads of information; to Michele Gale-Sinex for sustainable encouragement; and to Dhanu River for That Hat. Maximum thanks, though, to my husband Joe Eaton, who makes it not only possible but worth doing.

Table of Contents

INTRODUCTION

What Am I Doing Here?

What a great place to garden the Bay Area is! No hard dormant season to speak of, inspiration and examples everywhere, a tame-plant community as multicultural as the human one, a thousand reasons to play in the dirt. There are resources for gardeners springing up all over, as we add to our numbers. This book gathers as many of these resources as one mad gardener can track down, and lists them by area, to help you find those closest to you and to add one more temptation to stray from the freeway on local trips. It's about the great things we have here to garden with.

Gardening, like any art, is joyful echolocation, the outreach that tells us where we are, what we are, and the shape of things around us, while it advertises our own existence. This enterprise, in some form or other, is no more optional than vitamins in food. I get more substance and energy from my garden than I could from a super-duper supplement.

Somewhere in the real world (or in that interior climate where we can grow anything, spread our plots out over acres, and weed with our toes) there's a garden with a single unifying theme, its inhabitants grouped in a logical fashion, its purpose for existing plain to the educated eye. My garden will never be that sane. It's not that I'm indecisive (or am I?). I know what I want: everything. I want a drought-tolerant, lush, low-maintenance, all-native, exotic, basic, luxury, food, endangered-species reservoir, pure meditation garden, and I want it now. Oh yes, and no damned squirrels.

When I started gardening, I was a native plant purist. Except for the fava beans, and the tomatoes. What's the point of a garden without tomatoes? But other than that . . . oh, and maybe a little basil, rosemary . . . you know, mostly pure. What we had to work with then was a converted fish pond under a lot of Monterey pine and California laurel, filled in with mostly unamended soil, so it was like gardening on a brick in the bottom of a well. But the favas were happy: one tough plant, that. You see how things start creeping in.

Next house, I had a garden conveniently divided by the front walk, so it became droughty natives on one side and All Else on the other—food, herbs, Siberian iris, the Greek bay laurel, lilies. That helped organize both the care and the acquisitions, as I knew which holes were to be filled. That is, if a patch containing tomatoes, tradescantia, escaped mint, lavender (I forget why I put it on the watered side), lettuce, and giant zebra grass can be said to be organized at all.

My current garden won't be so easily divided. There's some shade on the sunny side, and sun in the summer-shady part, but only in winter, when the rest of the back is in deep moldy shade. (If you find that statement confusing, well, it should be.) There's a Japanese maple that preceded us in residence, so I have qualms about planting tomatoes—they can carry verticillium wilt—but I've done it anyway. There is a spot way in the back where plants drop dead for no apparent reason, though I haven't found any strange toxins in the soil; maybe it's just the worst of the bad drainage. Maybe it's bad juju. And one day the garage is going to fold in and sit down of its own accord like a trained elephant, so I shouldn't plant a tree where it would be hurt by whatever reconstruction we manage then. And there are flying soccer balls and too-vigorous volunteer plums and some mysterious grass I've never seen before. So far, every grand coherent plan has been accessorized with one or two very good reasons not to use it.

I watered a friend's garden while he was out of town and ran my fingers through his enviable dirt and watched the figs and grapefruit and cherries wake and blink and start to ripen on his trees. He's growing berries and carrots and greens and even potatoes there, all in raised beds with a few years of horse manure and compost to mellow the south Berkeley clay. I covet what he has, but I'm always barking my shins on raised beds; besides, the maple would resent that much cover dumped over her roots. Then again, what a luxury to have the stuff you can hardly buy at all, fresh and perfectly ripe a few feet from the kitchen.

Then I dropped in at the Tilden Park Botanic Garden, and the California azalea was in bloom, and right then I couldn't possibly want anything else but natives and the space to admire them.

Between these impulses, to grow dinner and to preserve rare plants, I've been brought up short by the question What am I doing when I'm gardening? I eat and feed, I conserve, I innovate and invent; I hide and reveal, I practice; sometimes, alas, I murder; other times I just fool around. I'm playing.

Even if you're a pro gardener, there's play at play in your work. I guess this, rather than scale or subject matter, is the difference between farming and gardening—in some sense, it's a luxury. We may garden as if our lives depended on it, but that's never more than half true. If you're shooting the moose in your cabbage patch and living strictly on moose-with-coleslaw, well, you're farming. (And hunting.) If you can farm with a sense of play, why, you're a Fully Realized Being, and my hat's off to you.

Play and pleasure are not dispensable, at least in my garden. I could probably survive on supermarket tomatoes if I had to, but if things are that strained I wouldn't bother with tomatoes at all. Styrotomatoes are pointless from every imaginable standpoint. So, is all the suspense and fertilizer worth it for a homegrown tomato? When you have the first one of the season in hand it doesn't matter anymore; as in good sex, judgment is suspended, irrelevant. No one needs a review or a grade, just a mouthful of tomato.

But there's that native azalea in Tilden, the sexiest shrub on earth with those golden white blooms in their rosy blush. I think so, at least until I brush past the Cleveland sage and its musky tang follows me for yards. Then the calochortus bed lifts its delicate cups to eye level in praise of dry, sunny, well-drained ground, and I walk into the redwood grove and a newborn, cool, moist exhalation embraces every inch of exposed skin. What could be better than a trillium? Couldn't I look at one every day? Isn't a native Californian garden what I really want? But fresh basil . . . my favorite fresh foods aren't native. Neither are those vaguely sinister succulents I keep falling for.

So I suppose I know what will happen after all: we'll all acquire plants and nudge around to find places for them; they'll be Californians and edibles and whims and gifts and castoffs; now and then we'll rearrange them to make more sense or live more amiably together. And I'm still looking around, and coming home with things I couldn't resist, and figuring out what to do with them: improv gardening.

While doing all this undisciplined unfocused garden browsing, I've learned a thing or two. One thing that feeds my arguable vice—wanting everything—is that just about everything is available here. We have limitations: fruits that need long winters with lots of chill won't bear well here, and semitropicals are a gamble, as we do have the odd frost. But there are people willing to push those boundaries, too, like California Rare Fruit Growers, and nurseries willing to indulge them. There are practitioners of dozens of regional garden traditions, from English borders to bonsai to French Intensive vegetable beds, who can teach and propagate and who support as many styles of associations and sellers. The climate (as well as the weather) makes it possible to earn a respectable living at gardening, and there are a number of schools where aspiring pros and amateurs can pick up skills, and where the ideas of each can cross-fertilize.

This book includes lists of several sorts of resources for gardeners in the Bay Area. There are clubs and associations, places to learn, ways to get your hands in the dirt even if you don't have any dirt to call your own; basic books to own or borrow; and places to buy plants and other necessities. Every resource is also a node of information about other resources;

expect to find things not in any book by way of things that *are* listed here. And I trust we'll all keep the information flowing, along with the saved seeds and cuttings. Bay Area gardeners have two major resources: this piece of the world and each other.

NOTE: I've included notes on wheelchair accessibility where possible. I don't use a chair myself and couldn't draft anyone who does to do a grand tour with me, so the notes represent only my own best guess, not measured engineering or test drives. Public meeting places, of course, can be reasonably expected to be accessible, and public gardens are becoming more reliable about it, if slowly. Nurseries and plant shops are as good a site as any commercial place for the messy collision of consciousness, conscience, budget, and space limitations. Some nurseries are situated on hillsides and terraces; some use a trailer with a couple of steps as an office; some have deeply mulched paths that are great soil treatment but can bog down wheels; some are just too crowded with plants to turn around in. And display tables are generally planned to work for an Average Person on foot. When I say "accessible," I am assuming the ability to negotiate a fairly hard unpaved surface, like a quarry-fines path, or mulch or gravel that's not very deep, and a bit of a slope. Other conditions are as noted.

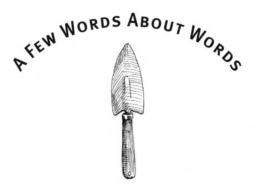

A FEW WORDS ABOUT WORDS

I've tried to minimize the jargon here because it gets obnoxious in large doses, particularly to a novice. But some of it is useful. Here are the working definitions of some of the odder words I and others use.

BULK SOILS AND OTHER BULK ITEMS: Soils, amendments (compost, manure, and such), gravel, sand, wood or bark chips, river rock or similar materials sold by the heap or truckload rather than in sacks. Since much of the price can be in the delivery fee, it saves considerably to take your pickup down to a place that sells bulk items and let them drop a cubic yard or so into it. It's also a lot cheaper than buying the same amount in bags.

CALIPER: The diameter of a tree trunk. This is also called "DBH" (diameter at breast height—four and a half feet from the ground) by pros and is a better indicator of a tree's strength and maturity than its height is.

COLOR: Nursery cant for plants, usually annuals, that give a quick hit of flower color to the garden. Also loosely called "bedding plants." Some pros with commercial accounts treat these as disposable; some people rotate them into and out of prominence in their own gardens. They're often the first thing you see when you walk into a retail nursery, all those impatiens and pansies and petunias in six-packs and jumbo six-packs and four-inch pots. They're the gardener's equivalent of a coffee break: not the sort of thing you want to live on as a steady diet, but just what you need when you need it.

CULTIVAR: A portmanteau word. It means a cultivated variety of a species. (See the sidebar "The Name of the Rosemary" on page 18 for one example.) In text and on properly grammatical labels, you'll see it in single quotation marks. All those roses named after presidents are cultivars.

HYDROPHOBIA: Not the old synonym for rabies, but a condition of soil or a soil substitute (like planting mix) that has dried out a lot and tends to float on water or let it run off unabsorbed. A soil mix with a lot of peat in it is likely to be hydrophobic, as are some local clay soils, which is why a first hard quick rain in fall doesn't soak in well.

IPM: Integrated Pest Management. In theory, this means keeping garden pests at a tolerable level by keeping plants healthy enough to shrug off most threats, and gardens friendly enough to local wildlife to allow, say, the birds to eat most of the bugs. When this fails, generally harmless substances like water—a blast from a hose will do a surprising amount of good—native or carefully evaluated imported predators, diseases that affect the pests, and least-toxic and very selective poisons, more or less in that order of preference, may be used. The idea is to substitute knowledge for heavy-handed bombing. Not everyone who talks about IPM actually practices it; it pays to ask about methods.

MALL BONSAI: The sort of thing some serious bonsai mavens sneer at, these are usually junipers, sometimes a shaped rosemary, or an untouched sago palm (there's not much you can do to shape a sago palm) in a rectangular pot. You see them in bonsai shops in malls, often with little ceramic clichés like arched bridges or people in robes stuck in their pots. The trees are usually not artistically done, as they are more or less mass-produced; it's not hard to get a good quick effect just by exposing the trunk of a common hedge juniper and putting it into a container that says, "This is a bonsai." I wouldn't consider these quintessential bonsai—for one thing, bonsai is something you do, not something you buy—but I don't think they're necessarily irredeemable junk either. Their hidden talent lies in getting someone interested in the art, which makes them a good gift; and they can be worked into interesting trees, given time and increasing skill. They tend to be affordable, and are usually a tough enough species to survive the learning experience.

SIZES: A four-inch perennial isn't necessarily four inches tall; the size refers to the top diameter of the pot it's in. A "#1" or one-gallon can refers to the nursery pots, usually black plastic and about eight inches tall, that most shrubs and perennials, and some other plants, are sold in. You'll see a very few of the old metal sort, still around from the days when they really were cans. There's an odd scissory implement called a red-top can-cutter that's used to get plants out of these, as the roots tend to cling to the rusting metal and to the ridges that give the can structural stability. The can-cutter is getting about as rare as the buttonhook, and for similar reasons.

SPECIMEN PLANT: One that's big and/or striking enough to hold center stage, to be a feature in a garden, to be the first thing you look at and say "Ah!" to when you walk in. It can be something inherently showy, like a magnolia in bloom, or something that's been beautifully shaped, like a pine done in bonsai style.

STANDARD: Two meanings in this book, and I've tried not to be too confusing. One, of course, is "normal" or "just this side of common." The other refers to a method of shaping plants: training to a standard means making what would generally be a shrub or vine stand up on an exposed trunk, often by tying it to a pole. This requires work, time, and an amenable plant, so the rose, camellia, or bougainvillea standards you see will likely be more expensive than their shrubby or viny kindred.

STARTS: Seedlings, starter-size plants.

VEGGIE: Vegetable, of course. There are those who wrinkle their noses at the nickname, but I use it—and I suspect others do too—because the word "vegetable" is a bit clumsy on the tongue and prone to unmusical slurrings.

A friend of mine, who is also a reformed Catholic and a gardener, used to squawk whenever I called a plant by its Latin name. Nostalgia aside, she heard it as pretense and obfuscation, though it was usually just the first thing that came to mind. I got my revenge the day she told me she'd graced her Thanksgiving turkey with wild sage. She'd gathered a native sagebrush, *Artemisia pycnocephala*, not at all a good substitute for culinary sage and not related to it, either. I took a base pleasure in telling her that if she'd been naming these plants properly, she'd have known an artemisia from a salvia, and wouldn't have been feeding her guests wormwood stuffing.

Even the stuff we don't grow ourselves needs its Latin name, especially in the average Bay Area multiculti kitchen. The Thai *kha* root you have is the Indonesian *laos* root you need, and they're both *Alpinia galanga*, which is why the Hong Kong label says "Galangal." If you're cutting corners or being creative, it helps to know it's in the ginger family, *Zingiberaceae*, whose Latin name is as zippy as its English one. And of course Chinese parsley, which isn't Chinese (it's a Mediterranean native), is almost always cilantro until it's old enough to be coriander, and there's a big difference between them. No help from Latin there; only cilantro's common name changes, and the only place it'll change into coriander is in the ground; in the fridge it ages into an appalling green slime rather too quickly. It helps to put it in a jar of water like a bouquet. Best is to grow it yourself directly from seed, and early; mine tends to bolt in summer, straight from seed leaves to attempted coriander seed.

The more adventurous a gardener you are, and the more varied your information sources, the more you'll find yourself looking up those official botanical names. I have learned, in gardening as in birding, to seek out the nearest little-old-lady-in-tennis-shoes and attach myself like a barnacle, in the hope of someday being one such myself. (A little old lady, not a barnacle.) Not all the good stuff has made it into the books yet. But the best learning isn't just receiving lore; it's also making connections, finding patterns, contributing to the flow. Digging up that bit of Latin opens the way to what everybody else in the world knows about a plant. Far from being a way to mystify, it can make it simpler to share what you learn with the widest possible audience.

I'm not, by the way, suggesting we forget common names; who could give up talking about puccoon? Naked ladies? Welcome-home-husband-but-never-so-drunk? (That's *Sedum acre*, and I don't know why.) We'd miss nodding toad, sticky monkeyflower, cow-itch, ear tree, Christ-in-a-hamper (which is Moses-in-a-boat), and fetid adder's-tongue. And pipsissewa, which really does exist outside the Uncle Wiggily continuum. There's a mustard relative in the Southwest called "tourist plant" because its seed-pods look like a little bitty pair of sunglasses; in California we have steers'-heads and elephants'-heads, and once you've seen them up close, you'll know why. And then there's the mysterious sand food. I'm given to naming things, myself, so every spring I'm out in the garden pulling out festering snotweed. You have to call it *something* until you get around to looking it up in *Hortus*.

If you can order sushi or dim sum, you can learn botanical names. They're quite systematic, and they reflect current understanding of how plants are related. What you usually see is the Latin binomial, e.g., *Arcto-staphylos pajaroensis*. Quite a mouthful, almost "Cornelius McGillicuddy."

Arctostaphylos is the genus and *pajaroensis* is the specific. It's arranged surname first (McGillicuddy, Cornelius), as it's part of a system that starts with the generic and moves to the species. The genus *Arcto-staphylos* includes all the manzanita species—some eighty-eight in California. One capitalizes only the genus. You may see a third name after the species; this is the subspecies or, if it's in single quotation marks, the variety. There's information in all this: *Arctostaphylos* means "bear grape"; *pajaroensis* suggests the species is found near the Pajaro River; the variety 'Myrtle Wolf' was named after a jewel of our local native plant enthusiasts' community, and honors both her and the plant.

LOCAL SALE EVENTS

Good advice for plant sales: wear your gardening clothes and shoes. Many of these sales take place on growing grounds, in nurseries, or in gardens, and you'll be dealing with recently watered gallon cans and probably with crowds, too. It's also a good idea to bring something to collect and carry your prizes in. A really sturdy carton, or a plastic, metal, or wooden crate will do; laundry baskets are usually not strong enough; one of those recycling bins you aren't supposed to use for anything but recycling would work really well, but of course it would never do for me to advise using one. At some sales, cash and personal checks are welcome but credit cards are not.

Sales of the sort listed here are good for unusual plants, for rare and endangereds whose provenance is blameless, for plants new to local gardens, and for heirlooms and specially bred varieties that will do well in our climate. Ask for advice on your purchases; sales are generally staffed and run by enthusiasts who want their plants to prosper and who love spreading knowledge.

I've also included in this section garden tours, paid or free, at which you can buy plants.

Most yearly sales are timed to coincide with one of our major planting seasons, spring and fall. In spring you get warm soil; in fall, free watering (assuming a "normal" rainy winter). It's typical to plant natives in the fall, both for the rain and, in some cases, because their roots are less resentful of the disturbance then. I like to use the fall planting season just to split the hard labor up a little.

MONTHLY SALES

STRYBING ARBORETUM SALE
Strybing Arboretum and Botanical Gardens
Ninth Avenue and Lincoln Way
Golden Gate Park
San Francisco
(415) 661-3090
Spring, summer, and fall
Saturdays 10 A.M.–1 P.M. Call for schedule.
The arboretum is mostly wheelchair accessible, with some steep slopes to beware of; not all paths are paved.

After the big general sales in early spring, the schedule shifts to individual plant types: natives, epiphyllums, and ferns, for example.

HEATHER FARM GARDEN CENTER MONTHLY PLANT SALE
Heather Farm Garden Center
1540 Marchbanks Drive
Walnut Creek
(510) 947-1678
First Wednesday of each month
9:30 A.M.–11:30 A.M.
Wheelchair accessible, with some slopes.

A variety of plants from the variety of gardens and garden associations here.

HALF MOON BAY COASTAL FLOWER MARKET

La Piazza Center
Kelly Avenue (between Main and Johnson)
Half Moon Bay
(650) 712-9439
Third Saturday of each month, except October
9 A.M.–3 P.M.

Festive street-fair sale; free parking.

SARATOGA HORTICULTURAL RESEARCH FOUNDATION MONTHLY PLANT SALE

15185 Murphy Avenue
San Martin
(408) 779-3303
First Friday of each month
9 A.M.–3 P.M.
Not wheelchair accessible

The Saratoga Foundation is a great source of new and newly discovered plant varieties well-adapted to Northern California climates. If you're looking for something elusive and special, or have the urge to be a year or two ahead of the horticultural crowd, it's worth the trip. It's worth the trip just to have a look at the place.

SPRING SALES

SAN FRANCISCO

BAMBOO FESTIVAL AND SALE

Northern California Chapter of the American Bamboo Society
San Francisco County Fair Building
Ninth Avenue and Lincoln Way
San Francisco
(415) 421-0930
April

Wheelchair accessible

Bamboo species, genera, and varieties typically unavailable through nurseries. Sales and auction, arts and crafts exhibits, music, and more.

DAHLIA SOCIETY OF CALIFORNIA ANNUAL TUBER SALE
San Francisco County Fair Building
Ninth Avenue and Lincoln Way
San Francisco
(415) 566-5222
First Saturday in April
Wheelchair accessible

Dahlias of all sorts, many from the demonstration garden near the conservatory in Golden Gate Park, and all properly aged-off and lableled. Help and expert advice, too.

SAN FRANCISCO LANDSCAPE GARDEN SHOW
Cow Palace
San Francisco
(415) 750-5108
April
Admission fee benefits Golden Gate Park
Wheelchair accessible

Lots of unusual plants and accompaniments for sale; ideas and information are mostly free for the taking, though there are some workshops with separate admission charges. Generally crowded. Food and drink are available.

ANNUAL SPRING SALE
Strybing Arboretum and Botanical Gardens
Ninth Avenue and Lincoln Way
San Francisco
(415) 661-3090
May
Wheelchair accessible

Members-only sale Friday, and public sale Saturday. This is a bigger deal than Strybing Arboretum's monthly sales, and is likely to have a wider variety of plants.

ORCHIDMANIA'S WORLD'S LARGEST ORCHID GARAGE SALE
Nihonmachi Center
Post and Buchanan Streets
San Francisco
(415) 558-8444
http://www.orchids.org
Mother's Day Weekend
Wheelchair accessible

OrchidMania's excellent sales benefit grassroots AIDS prevention and relief organizations in the United States, Central America, and Southeast Asia. They also have the good effect of propagating endangered orchid species; the orchids on sale are donated by growers here and abroad, or are propagated by OrchidMania's own orchidmaniacs. The Mother's Day sale includes talks and potting demonstrations. Other sales take place now and then, too. There's a fall sale in Berkeley, for example; call or check out OrchidMania's Web site for announcements. For OrchidMania's mailing address, see page 95 of Plant and Garden Societies chapter.

EAST BAY

MAMMOTH BONSAI BAZAAR
Lakeside Park Garden Center
666 Bellevue Avenue
Oakland
(510) 569-8003 (ask for Bill Castellon)
Last Sunday in February
Wheelchair accessible

Fund-raising sale of bonsai and bonsai-related things benefits the Northern

California Bonsai Collection, in its new home at Lake Merritt in Oakland. Demonstrations and workshops, too.

ANNUAL CALIFORNIA HORTICULTURAL SOCIETY PLANT SALE
Lakeside Park Garden Center
666 Bellevue Avenue
Oakland
(415) 566-5222
March
Wheelchair accessible

Thousands of rare and unusual plants grown by members or donated by nurseries.

OPEN DAY IN THE GARDEN
The Ruth Bancroft Garden
Walnut Creek
(510) 210-9663
April
$7, free to members
Wheelchair accessible

Grand springtime opening includes docent tours, plant sale, and refreshments. Reservations required. Call for details.

SPRING NATIVE PLANT SALE AT TILDEN PARK
Tilden Regional Park Botanic Garden
Wildcat Canyon Road at South Park Drive
Berkeley
Early April, usually the Saturday nearest to Earth Day
10 A.M.–3 P.M.
Partly wheelchair accessible, but not easy; steep grassy slopes in some of the sale area can be slippery even to walk on.

Native plants, many rare and endangered, none boring. The sale is put on by a dedicated group of volunteers that has recently become the Friends of the

Tilden Park Botanic Garden (see page 92). Proceeds benefit the garden directly, since these marvelous fanatics donate their time to propagate the plants.

SPRING PLANT SALE
Markham Regional Arboretum
West end of La Vista Avenue, one-half mile off Clayton Road
Concord
(510) 486-1550
April
Wheelchair accessible

Plants from specialty growers (geraniums, Mediterranean plants), California natives, and drought-resistant plants.

UC BOTANICAL GARDEN SPRING PLANT SALE
University of California Botanical Garden
200 Centennial Drive
Berkeley
(510) 643-2755
http://www.mip.berkeley.edu/garden/
April
Friday members-only sale and Saturday public sale.
Partly wheelchair accessible; steep slopes abound.

Unusual plants from around the world; good advice.

A CELEBRATION OF OLD ROSES SHOW AND SALE
Heritage Roses Group
El Cerrito Community Center
Moeser Lane (at Ashbury)
El Cerrito
May
(510) 254-0319
Wheelchair accessible

Festive, celebratory, charming event with lots of distractions.

FIESTA DE LAS FLORES

Diablo Valley College Horticulture Department Nursery
321 Golf Club Road
Pleasant Hill
(510) 685-1230 ext. 443 or ext. 478
May, before Mother's Day, a Saturday
Wheelchair accessible, though tight spaces

Plant sale and celebration: art, book signings, slides, talks, and demonstrations.

FLATLAND FLOWER FARM

Annual Open Garden and Plant Sale
1126 Blake Street (near San Pablo)
Berkeley
(510) 843-7523
Early May, usually a Sunday
Sale area—the driveway—is wheelchair accessible, but can be crowded. The garden is approachable by chair, with the caution that paths are deeply mulched and tight in part of it.

Small sale by a small business with an inspiring small garden. Anyone who gardens in bayside flatlands clay will find even the dirt here exciting, and under the fruit trees and climbing roses you'll see the prettiest breed of chickens on earth; they're called Millefleurs. The sale is apt to run heavily to old roses and sunflowers, old-fashioned cottage garden flowers, and edibles, particularly herbs. You can often find Flatland flowers and starts at the Berkeley Farmers' Markets.

MERRITT COLLEGE SPRING PLANT SALE

Merritt College Campus
Landscape Horticulture Department
12500 Campus Drive
Oakland
(510) 436-2418

May
Wheelchair accessible

Rare and unusual plants, many new introductions, gourmet vegetable starts, annuals, garden sculpture, and more. Lots of help and information, and food and drink.

ORCHID SOCIETY OF CALIFORNIA ANNUAL SALE
Lakeside Park Garden Center on Lake Merritt
666 Bellevue Avenue
Oakland
(510) 839-9647 (ask for Ray Vickers)
Mother's Day weekend
Wheelchair accessible

Sale of user-friendly orchids by an equally friendly group. Lots of tips and advice available, from hobby growers and commercial propagators, including the brand-new Adams Point Orchids.

NORTH BAY

INVERNESS GARDEN CLUB PRIMROSE TEA
The Dance Palace
Point Reyes Station
(415) 663-8977
March
Wheelchair accessible
Nominal admission fee

Plant sale, as well as tea, Victorian-style, and other goings-on. Wear your flowered hat.

PENINSULA

WILDFLOWER SHOW AND NATIVE PLANT SALE

California Native Plant Society, Santa Clara Valley Chapter
Foothill College
El Monte Road
Los Altos Hills
(650) 856-7579
April
Campus is mostly wheelchair accessible.
Beware! Parking permit machine requires eight quarters.

Native plants that will thrive in the South Bay, expert advice, and carefully chosen wildflowers to look at and be inspired.

ANNUAL GAMBLE SPRING GARDEN TOUR

The Elizabeth F. Gamble Garden Center
1431 Waverley Street
Palo Alto
(650) 329-1356, FAX (650) 329-1688
First Friday and Saturday in May, 10 A.M.–4 P.M.
Wheelchair accessible

Self-guided tour of private gardens, plus a springtime look at the Gamble Garden Center. Plant clinic by UC master gardeners; sales of garden goods, plants, and seedlings; silent auction; tea and cookies offered throughout the day.

Box lunches are available; reservations required. Call or fax the numbers above for questions and reservations. Tour fee about $20 to $25.

SOUTH BAY

UC SANTA CRUZ ARBORETUM ASSOCIATES HUMMINGBIRD FESTIVAL

UCSC Arboretum

1156 High Street
Santa Cruz
(408) 427-2998
March

Hummingbird-attracting plants and other hummingbird-related items for sale; tours and videos.

THE FLEA MARKET
Annual Spring in Guadalupe Gardens Fair
Guadalupe River Park and Gardens
Spring and Taylor Streets
San Jose
(408) 298-7657
April
Wheelchair accessible

The master gardeners of Santa Clara County, the South Bay Heritage Rose Group, and the Guadalupe River Park and Gardens collaborate on a diversified sale.

SPRING PLANT SALE
Santa Cruz Chapter of the California Native Plant Society and UCSC Arboretum
Arboretum Eucalyptus Grove on High Street
UC Santa Cruz
(408) 475-9653
April

The eucalyptus grove location is ironic, but the sale is a gold mine.

CABRILLO COLLEGE ANNUAL PLANT SALE
Cabrillo College
6500 Soquel Drive
Aptos
(408) 469-6100
Mother's Day weekend, Friday through Sunday; members' preview on the preceding Thursday.

School sales are often a good source of both tough standbys and esoteric plants new to or not yet in the trade.

FALL SALES

EAST BAY

AFRICAN VIOLET SOCIETY OF DIABLO VALLEY
Heather Farm Garden Center
1540 Marchbanks Drive
Walnut Creek
(510) 751-6037
October
Wheelchair accessible

Unusual breeds of violets, and help with growing them.

ANNUAL IRIS SALE
Open Day in the Garden: Ruth Bancroft Garden
The Ruth Bancroft Garden
Walnut Creek
(510) 210-9663
October, a Saturday afternoon
Wheelchair accessible
Docent tours, plants sale, and refreshments

Reservations are required, and there's a fee (under $10) for admission, unless you're a member. It's worth it just for a look at this extraordinary garden.

CALIFORNIA NATIVE PLANT SOCIETY, EAST BAY CHAPTER
Annual Native Plant Sale
CNPS Growing Grounds
Merritt College Landscape Horticulture Department
12500 Campus Drive

Oakland
(510) 376-4095 or (510) 559-9269
Early October, Saturday and Sunday
Mostly wheelchair accessible, but some areas are deeply mulched, boggy,
or sloping.

This is a big one: thousands of native plants, all scrupulously labeled; bulbs, seeds, art, books, clothing, and free expert advice. Usual starting time is 10 A.M., and it's a good idea to get there early, as you can learn a lot just standing in line and eavesdropping on the professionals and passionate amateurs who patronize this sale.

MERRITT COLLEGE FALL PLANT SALE
Merritt College Landscape Horticulture Department
Courtyard—inside the department building
12500 Campus Drive
Oakland
(510) 436-2418
An early October Saturday and Sunday, 9 A.M.–3 P.M.
Wheelchair accessible

A rare doubleheader, same days and same place as the CNPS sale. Here's where to get your fall veggie starts, exotics, some fruit trees, and things unexpected and gorgeous in general. There's more expert advice here, too, and food and drink for sale.

DIABLO VALLEY COLLEGE FALL PLANT SALE
Diablo Valley College Horticulture Department Nursery
321 Golf Club Road
Pleasant Hill
(510) 685-1230 ext. 443 or ext. 478
Usually November, but DVC has held its fall sale on various dates; call in early fall to be sure.
Wheelchair accessible; tight spaces

Unusual and climate-conscious plants.

NORTH BAY

FALL NATIVE PLANT SALE
California Native Plant Society, Milo Baker (Sonoma) Chapter
Luther Burbank Art and Garden Center
2050 Yulupa Avenue
Santa Rosa
(707) 833-2856
October
Wheelchair accessible

Worth a trip to see what this interesting chapter of CNPS has been up to.

There are gardeners who drop their garden-porn magazines and seed catalogues on the odd sunny hour in the gray dead of winter, to step outside and tuck a few of last year's hoarded seeds and rooted cuttings into a sheltered, snailproof spot in the garden, careful of course not to trample the soggy soil. Then there are gardeners like me.

In winter my garden is a swamp of guilt. The Douglas iris is mangy, the flannelbush looks moribund again, the back forty is under water, and the snails are sliming the chard. Yecch. I don't want to put a finger in the cold cold ground; I don't even want to look at it. If it's not raining, I'd rather be out in the Real World chasing the waterfowl and fancy raptors while they're here. A winter landscape should at least have a good bird in it, but despite the standing water I haven't yet managed to lure a sandhill crane to my yard.

Raising a piece of the Real World is one thing I'm trying to do in the garden, to reproduce a taste of the wild stuff I can't live without. But in winter, the birds beyond my garden are the best access to that world: every time I go out somewhere and watch them I learn more and renew my own connection to things living. In short, the reason I garden at all is the reason I'm not gardening in January.

But in February, something green in me creaks open when the plums start to bloom. I wish I'd planted bulbs last November. I wish I'd started tomato seeds in pots last month. I wish I had a flunky to pull the Kikuyu grass. I wish I had more backyard and more foresight. While I'm still wishing, and admiring the gardens of the industrious, it turns into March and April and only my garden's bones—the ceanothus and such—are blooming.

But I'll catch up. There will be impulse buys, and rooted cuttings, and orphans, and gifts. Something will get the urge to outgrow its allotted space. Somehow, without much planning, by June there won't be a patch of bare dirt left. The garden is exuberant; even the weeds look less sinister.

In late summer, a gardener of native plants learns to love seedheads and sage leaves, and the grace of blown bunchgrasses. The native part of the garden gilds itself; the irrigated veggie patch begins to look as artificial as Astroturf. Time—seasonality—is as important a dimension in a garden as depth and elevation. The same changes that might remind us, to our regret, of the mortality we share with all live things also make a garden more than a museum room or an exercise in decorating. Hardscape is all very well, but it's the fleeting, exasperating, surprising life that makes a garden.

PUBLIC GARDENS

SAN FRANCISCO

GOLDEN GATE PARK
San Francisco
Park information: (415) 666-7200
AIDS Memorial Grove information: (415) 750-8340
Japanese Tea Garden hours and fees: (415) 666-7107

There are a number of gardens hidden and incorporated in this biggest garden in San Francisco; the Japanese tea garden, next to the current museum complex, charges an admission fee. There's a Shakespeare garden—there's no end to gardeners' odd organizing principles—near the museums, Strybing Arboretum (see below), and the badly injured Conservatory of Flowers, whose surround of flowerbeds is still intact. There's a garden of mite-resistant fuchsias, a rose garden, a rhododendron dell.

There are also surprises like a buffalo paddock, artificial waterfalls and streams, a tree fern grove worthy of predinosaurian inhabitants, and interesting plantings scattered all over. An AIDS Memorial Grove stands near the Stanyan Street park entrance.

STRYBING ARBORETUM AND BOTANICAL GARDENS
Ninth Avenue at Lincoln Way (Golden Gate Park)
San Francisco
(415) 661-1316
Weekdays 8 A.M.–4:30 P.M.
Weekends, holidays 10 A.M.–5 P.M.
Mostly wheelchair accessible; there are some steep-looking slopes. Most paths are paved.

Known to area birders as well as gardeners, Strybing's plants from Chile, New Zealand, Australia, Asia, South Africa, and a "New World cloud forest" may be what attract birds from way out of range in winter. There are also rock gardens, a Japanese moon garden, gardens of primitive plants, California natives, redwoods, extraordinary magnolias, scented herbs, rarely seen trees, proteas, succulents, and more. Quite an education, or just a nice place for a stroll, a sit, or a look at the ducks.

EAST BAY

BERKELEY MUNICIPAL ROSE GARDEN
1201 Euclid Avenue (at Bay View Place)
Berkeley
(510) 644-6530
Wheelchair accessible, but there are iffy slopes.

More than just a deer smorgasbord, this amphitheater of roses (designed, no doubt, to give the plants a splendid bay view) is a great place to stroll, inhale, window-shop, or just sit. It's a popular wedding site and is being rendered wheelchair accessible. It's also a favorite spot to view Fourth of July fireworks; get there early for a good seat.

TILDEN PARK BOTANIC GARDEN
Wildcat Canyon Road and South Park Drive
Berkeley
(510) 841-8732
Daily 8:30 A.M.–5 P.M.
Partly wheelchair accessible; steep slopes.

An excellent botanical microcosm of California spread out over acres of gracious slopes and meanders. It's a great place for a stroll; you never quite know where you'll end up. The redwood grove is the place to be on the rare hot day in Berkeley. Plants are conscientiously labeled, and grouped by place of origin, a simple but startlingly effective design scheme. The garden is a gene bank as well as an education: endemic, rare and endangered plants join garden favorites and esoteric mountaintop dwellers. Talks and slide shows about California's unique plants and places, and adventures therein, take place on weekends and some evenings, in fall and winter; call for the schedule.

UNIVERSITY OF CALIFORNIA BOTANICAL GARDEN
Centennial Drive
Berkeley
(510) 642-3343
Daily 9 A.M.–4:45 P.M.
Closed Christmas Day
Summer hours may vary.
Thursdays free; otherwise, $3 general admission unless you're a UC student.
Partly wheelchair accessible; steep graveled slopes.

The admission charge is new; there's already a charge to park in the lot across the road, but you can take the UC shuttle from the Berkeley BART station into Strawberry Canyon as it goes up to the Lawrence Hall and Lab. There's something here for everyone, including newt watchers. Don't miss the Weltwitschia in the cacti-and-succulents house near the entrance, or the rainforest house down the hill. You probably won't get a chance to grow a Weltwitschia at home, but its frazzled endurance is inspiring. The California natives area segues neatly into the oak woodland that surrounds the garden, with a side trip into eastern North America for us transplants to reminisce in. Every continent but Antarctica is represented here, and I can't wait to see how they'll pull that one off. The view at dusk is worth the trip.

MARKHAM REGIONAL ARBORETUM
West end of La Vista Avenue, one-half mile off Clayton Road
Concord
(510) 486-1550
Daily 8 A.M. to dusk
The arboretum and community garden area are wheelchair accessible, the natural creekside less so, though it's approachable in places, for instance at the bridge.

Concentrates on native California and Mediterranean-climate plants, but other foci are being developed. This garden's still a fledgling, but already hosts a thriving community garden, protects a productive little riparian strip of wildland, and is growing other formal and demonstration gardens. It'll be interesting to watch it mature.

BLAKE ESTATE GARDEN
70 Rincon Road
Kensington
(510) 524-2449
Monday–Friday 8 A.M.–4:30 P.M.
Mostly wheelchair accessible

Italianate garden, a classic with some interesting turns, well laid-out views, walks, specimens, formal and informal spaces. Don't miss the walk through the woods on the north end of the lot, a well-done transition from the manicured to the apparently wild. Look closely; the "wild" side is as carefully built and managed as the formal pool and bay view gardens.

DUNSMUIR HOUSE AND GARDEN

2960 Peralta Oaks Park

Oakland

(510) 615-5555

Garden is wheelchair accessible.

Grounds are open to the public free of charge Tuesday through Friday from 10 A.M. to 4 P.M., April to September. House and garden tours are offered on Wednesdays and some Sundays for a modest fee; there are occasional special events. Available for weddings and such ceremonies, the grand old house and gardens enclose good strolling space, and the gardens boast some splendid specimen trees.

FIRESTORM MEMORIAL GARDEN

Hiller Drive and Tunnel Road

Oakland

(510) 843-3828

Wheelchair accessible; mostly to be viewed from the sidewalk.

A good example of a mostly water-thrifty garden that looks lush and colorful much of the year, this is also a fairly contemplative space, which is quite an achievement in this heavily trafficked spot. Part of this is thanks to the elevation; put yourself high enough above a freeway confluence and it does take on some of the character of a river. Part is due to the splendid bay and cities view, opened up by the 1991 Oakland Hills fire's consumption of most of the surrounding eucalyptus. (I used to like those trees; they danced with tensile grace in the prevailing wind, and taught me what the species was good at.) The placement of water-loving plants at the foot of the drinking fountain is deft, and the masses and drifts of short herbaceous and woody perennials are encouraging while managing to be relatively fire-safe. The North Hills Landscape Committee, responsible for the memorial, is working at lining the surrounding roadside with fire-resistant plants, and it will be interesting to watch both the original garden and the fire-resistant demo garden develop (the latter is now just a hopeful billboard on a certainly fire-resistant, scraped patch), both in terms of design and as an indicator of political will and civic memory.

And I think May Blos would have liked some of the extensive use of California native plants in the memorial.

LAKESIDE PARK GARDENS

666 Bellevue Avenue
Oakland
(510) 238-3208 (Park Service)
Weekdays 10 A.M.–3 P.M.
Saturday and Sunday 10 A.M.–4 P.M.
Wheelchair accessible

A variety of demonstration gardens—from multicultural community vegetable gardens to iris, palm, scent, herb, succulent, traditional Japanese (a gift of Oakland's sister city Fukuoka) and various plant showcases—and the new home of the Northern California Bonsai Collection. The Garden Center building includes meeting and show space, and hosts a garden library you can join for two dollars a year, open Thursdays.

MORCOM AMPHITHEATER OF ROSES

700 Jean Street
Oakland
(510) 238-3187 (Oakland Parks and Recreation Department)
Daily dawn to dusk
Mostly wheelchair accessible; one section is up a pretty steep slope.

Oakland's official rose garden is a stately collection, mostly of hybrid tea roses, in a natural bowl with lots of strolling room. There's a children's rose garden, all of dwarf roses; a Mother's Walk, lined with bronze plaques that honor Oakland's Mothers of the Year; and pools, some fed by a waterfall fountain. The roses are labeled meticulously, though vandals have done away with a few of the tags. The WPA/Italianate architecture of the gateway, the service building, and the pools is handsome and relaxing, and there's a wisteria at the entrance that's glorious in bloom. To reserve the garden for a wedding or other ceremony, call the Parks and Rec number above.

PROJECT YES GARDENS
Oakland

Youth Engaged in Service sponsors six composting demonstration gardens at Oakland schools: Claremont Middle School, Frick Junior High, John Swett School, Oakland High, Washington Elementary, and Westlake Junior High. If you want to visit any of them, contact Cathleen Michaels at the East Bay Conservation Corps (510) 891-3917.

HEATHER FARM GARDEN CENTER
1540 Marchbanks Drive
Walnut Creek
(510) 947-6712
Daily dawn to dusk
Office and library open daily 9 A.M.–1 P.M.
Wheelchair accessible; some slopes, but paths are winding and graded well.

Sometimes the parking lot is closed to the public, during weddings, for example, but there's lots of curbside parking on the block. The ongoing project of a coalition of local civic and garden organizations, Heather Farm (the eponymous Heather was a horse) contains a butterfly garden, a California native garden, a children's garden, a rock garden, a sensory garden, and a mural garden. Get the picture? There's a compost project, too, and it's a good place to learn techniques. Besides its didactic uses, the garden's a nice rambly walk. The streamside strip is a blend of formal-exotic and informal-native, with daylilies and vine maples and local trees integrated pretty well in a shallow space. There's an open space, surrounded by roses, around a handsome gazebo where weddings can be held; the garden center building can be rented, too, for the reception. Many garden and plant societies use Heather Farm as a meeting and sales space; the center itself has major sales in spring and fall.

LINDSAY MUSEUM NATURE GARDEN

1931 First Avenue
Walnut Creek
(510) 935-8015
Open daylight hours; admission to the garden is free.
Wheelchair accessible

The museum charges a modest fee and is open Wednesday through Sunday, 11 A.M. to 5 P.M. It's worth dropping in there with the kids; Lindsay does wildlife rehab (and teaches it, along with other natural history subjects, to adults and youngsters) and displays animals it can't release. The garden is a nicely planned native-plant display, water-thrifty and relaxing to be in.

RUTH BANCROFT GARDEN

Walnut Creek
(510) 210-9663
Call for directions and reservations.
Friday and Saturday garden tours, spring, summer, and fall. Modest fee and reservations required.
Wheelchair accessible

An extraordinary garden that's heavy on the dry-adapted plants and gorgeously laid out. It's possibly the best place to see the Antioch Dunes evening primrose, a local rare and endangered plant, and any number of succulents, trees, California natives, and exotics from Australia and other Mediterranean-climate regions. Currently under the care of the novel Garden Conservancy, a private enterprise version of Britain's National Trust and an idea whose time has come.

INLAND MENDOCINO EXPEDITION

It's only about two hours' drive to get to Hopland on Route 101 and, once you get past the crowded Marin-Santa Rosa corridor, the ride's quite pleasant. There are two major attractions for gardeners there: the Fetzer Winery gardens and Real Goods' new Solar Living Center. (There's also good food at the Bluebird Cafe and at Mendocino Brewery's pub.)

Fetzer has put together an inspired set of gardens around its tasting room/deli/B&B complex. Handsome gray stonework sets off thriving perennial beds, worth a long look for some eye-pleasing combinations and for water-thriftiness in general. Stroll a little farther, and you'll be walking through a perfectly gorgeous kitchen garden, much of it handily labeled, full of heirloom and newfangled experimental fruits and vegetables: berries, greengages, salads, herbs, and, oh, all sorts of tasty-looking things, arranged along rows and concentric paths with the occasional posted piety about biodiversity and explanations of what's going on here. I'm passionate about biodiversity myself—as I am about anything forestalling the McDonald'sization of the world—and am pleased to see Fetzer's folks walking their talk here.

Right on 101 in Hopland, at the south end of town, you'll see the Real Goods store, whose Solar Living Center is such a great big deal they offer guided tours. You can have a self-guided tour, too; there's a rack of brochures between the parking lot and the store. I get itchy when faced with a lot of concentrated virtue, including virtue of the environmental sort, but this place is enough of a forebrain funhouse to slide its obvious good works into pure gladness. There are enough bright ideas here, from the waterworks to the interplanted fat-hipped roses and cordoned fruit trees to the willow dome and hops tepee, to give any gardener the grins. Wander the grounds, spiral up to the summit fountain—the fountains here are possibly the most elegant I've seen anywhere, while almost cornily down-home—and don't miss the restrooms. Particularly, don't miss the wainscoting in the restrooms. Bring the kids; there's a terrific sandbox. Wait till you see the tricks these folks make trees do. They run classes in a lot of the techniques used to such good effect here; ask for a schedule.

Seasoned Californians know those lion-colored hills we watch nervously all summer and fall are as much an artifact as the roads winding through them. We all know that eucalyptus groves are no more native than my Toyota, and yellow broom is just another noxious weed. Right? Much of the alleged California landscape is a patchwork of imports; we'd need a time machine to get back to nature if we meant by that anything aboriginal. How on earth did this happen?

Gardeners are to blame for a lot of it, I cringe to admit: the respectable lawns, the willows and forsythia imported from back East so our gardens would look gardeny. I confess I have a spindly little lilac in my yard.

Most of this stuff is harmless, if homely. But some of it can actually be dangerous, when it gets loose and gallops off into the wildlands.

The brooms were imported over a century ago by a San Francisco nursery, and are still being sold as easy, drought-tolerant plants. That they are; they're also a fire hazard. Broom has a nastier cousin, gorse; there's some debate as to whether that one was imported on purpose or not. Gorse is a grungy, thorny shrub; it's hard to imagine anyone liking it enough to plant it.

Possibly the evilest ornamental is tamarisk. It's graceful; it's droughty; it sends roots far and deep and sucks up all the water in (or out of) sight. This makes it a menace to desert oases, pools, and even perennial streams. It makes poor forage and shelter, and outcompetes natives (partly by secreting salt crystals and salting the soil around it), so it's a double threat to wildlife.

Other garden escapes that threaten wild plants or just plain get out of hand here are ivy (English and German), vinca, Capeweed, *Pennisetum* grasses, that pestilential Bermuda buttercup (which is not a buttercup and not from Bermuda), nasturtium, Bermuda grass and Kikuyu grass, and the weed trees *Ailanthus altissima* and acacias.

The weediest weed tree here, blue gum eucalyptus, was the focus of a nineteenth-century land improvement scheme. It was touted as a source of honey, insecticides, pulp, medicine, fuel, and lumber, and dominated 65,000 acres of the state by 1900. The lumber was unworkable and fragile; the other uses were bypassed by technology; the leftover trees stayed on and prospered, and lots of people today think they're natives. Bees still like them, as do monarch butterflies and hummingbirds, but a grove of eucalypti doesn't support anything like the live diversity of a grove of oaks. Seems they're everywhere; once I heard a radio person refer to a concert by the "Eucland Oath Chorus." I want to hear them swear.

Pampas grass was an industry for a while, too: between 1872 and 1895, the Goleta Valley (Santa Barbara County) supplied Victorian parlors with its feathery flowers. It's also been used for landscaping and for dune stabilization. *Cortaderia selloana* isn't a big problem; its rattier, sturdier sibling species, *C. jubata,* is what swarms all over the sea cliffs and invades forests.

Many of our landscape pests followed Europeans here for more practical reasons: food and pharmaceuticals. Everyone needed English plantain and yarrow for poultices, watercress to prevent scurvy, mullein for sore throats (and for tinder and lamp wicks), and shepherd's purse for earache. Mustard was for poultices as well as for seasoning; it showed up here long before baseball and hot dogs. The Franciscans are supposed to have strewn it, parable fashion, along the mission trail to mark the way. Now, of course, the whole landscape is plastered with it, and anyone using it for road signs would be following the scenic route to West Upthecreek.

Chicory and dandelion have roots that roast up into "coffee," and dandelion greens are edible. That's why they're here. (I had a nasty dandelion wine once, which is why I don't consider it a delicacy. Imagine alcoholic prune juice.) Himalayan blackberry, a pest of yard and wildland, arrived as a food source, as did the fennel along the roads and wetlands, and the big, electric-blue-flowered cardoon in the local parks. So did the snails we all know and love. Inadvertent imports and garden escapes are still happening; I looked around for escaped onion lily, or wild chives.

Other invaders hitched rides with useful stuff. Those tindery grasses around us traveled economy class in the guts of livestock, and as seeds in their fodder. Thistle seeds are small and hard to sort out of commercial seed batches. Good old tumbleweed is actually Russian, a native of the steppes, maybe a contaminant of flax seed. Yellow star thistle shows up in scary quantities along roads and in fields well up into the mountains, and poisons horses that incautiously graze it. Ships once used soil as ballast, and dumped it as landfill and roadbeds, along with whatever was dormant in it. And any plant moved with its rootball intact might have seedy company. Once on the continent, weed seeds, mobile and tenacious, migrated via wind, water, fur, clothing, tracked mud, railroad, and car fender to land in our gardens, from which we donate them to our friends' gardens, and so it goes. The second human landing party on Mars will probably find sow thistle underfoot.

NORTH BAY

MARIN ART AND GARDEN CENTER
30 Sir Francis Drake Boulevard
Ross
OFFICE:
  Monday–Friday 9 A.M.–4 P.M.
  (415) 454-5597
ROSS GARDEN RESTAURANT:
  Tuesday–Friday 11:30 A.M.–2 P.M.
  (415) 456-7870
JOSE MOYA DEL PINO LIBRARY, ART AND GARDEN BOOKS:
  Tuesday–Friday 11 A.M.–3 P.M.
DECORATIONS GUILD SHOP:
  Monday–Friday 10 A.M.–4 P.M.
  First Saturday every month noon–4 P.M.
  (415) 454-5720
RENTALS: LIVERMORE ROOM:
  (415) 454-1301
FRANCES YOUNG ART GALLERY:
  Monday–Thursday 11 A.M.–4 P.M. Saturday, Sunday noon–4 P.M.
  (415) 454-9561
ROSS VALLEY PLAYERS BOX OFFICE:
  (415) 456-9555
LAUREL HOUSE ANTIQUE SHOP
  Monday 10–2, Tuesday–Friday 11 A.M.–4 P.M. Saturday 11 A.M.–2 P.M.
  Consignments taken Monday 10 A.M.–1 P.M.
  (415) 454-8472

Busy, busy, busy. Behind that wavy brick wall, the Marin Art and Garden Center (yes, the acronym's pronounced "magic") hosts a film series, a Spring Flower Festival, a Spring Fair, Market Day, a Strawberry Faire, an Alfresco Luncheon Fashion series, an art auction, a greens sale, and a bake sale—all annual—plus weddings and children's parties. Festivities aside, this is a place to enjoy the company of several *grande dame* trees, in particular an arresting magnolia that is forming her own forest in a round green lawn, and a *Sequoiadendron*, the Sierran Big Tree, behind her. Among the interesting trees and plants are equally interesting structures, in particular the Bottle House (nothing like Grandma Prisbie's, but elf-craftsman handsome) and the Octagon House. The paths lead visitors on a pleasant meander through examples of spacious and compact, loose and formal styles.

PENINSULA

ALLIED ARTS GUILD
75 Arbor Road at Cambridge
Menlo Park
(650) 326-3632, information
(650) 324-2588, lunch reservations at the Allied Arts Restaurant
Monday–Saturday 10 A.M.–5 P.M.
Wheelchair accessible

A public garden with retail shops; sales benefit the pediatric hospital at Stanford. See page 175 for more information.

SUNSET DEMONSTRATION GARDEN
Lane Publishing
80 Willow Road (at Middlefield)
Menlo Park
(650) 321-3600
Monday–Friday 9 A.M.–4:30 P.M.

Don't try to drive around the block for a better view, or you'll end up in the next town and heading in the wrong direction entirely. I believe Menlo Park keeps its chronosynclastic infundibulum next door to the *Sunset* publishing headquarters. The building isn't obvious at all from the street, but once you're through the imposing California-colonial doors, you'll be made welcome in a low-key way, exemplified by the big pot of black umbrellas for rainy-day tourists. The garden is a self-guided tour: lots of handsome plants, well-labeled and surrounding an obscene expanse of lawn. Some of the trees around the lawn are native live oaks, and clearly not happy in their wet-footed situation. If you start out widdershins on the path, the first thing you come to is an example of heroic surgery and its limitations; this live oak has been treated and cauterized and filled with Styrofoam. It looks like a burn victim—a stately, valiant burn victim. Veer to the right, and you'll find a tiny, busy home-style garden patch where *Sunset* staff raises samples of the plants that figure in the coming year's magazine features. In my guise as mild-mannered magazine columnist I chatted with the head of this department, who mentioned that he uses organic methods here. The rest of the route around the lawn displays perennials, trees, and shrubs, in-filled with annuals in season, all (except for the live oaks) looking happy and well-trimmed. If you peer or slip backstage, you'll see San Francisquito Creek, merry in winter, bone-dry in summer, and one reason for the garden's interesting birdlife. What the place needs here is a deck or designated overlook for the creek; even when it's dry it's a strong natural presence.

THE ELIZABETH F. GAMBLE GARDEN CENTER
1431 Waverley Street
Palo Alto
(650) 329-1356
FAX (650) 329-1688
Wheelchair accessible

The admonition not to touch (or pick) the plants here is understandable, but they don't make it easy; there's one whole garden devoted just to sages. In addition, there are beds of herbs; pelargoniums *and* geraniums (adjacent, to show the difference); perennials for cutting; a mostly white rose garden; the master gardeners' demo garden (whose changing cast is reliably handsome); the Roots and Shoots Intergenerational Program's lush produce patch (complete with scarecrows); allées; fountains; strolls; every sort of inspiring space. There is even a population of rather handsome melanistic squirrels.

The Gamble Center (as in Proctor and Gamble) is a turn-of-the-century estate deeded to the city by the first inhabitants' daughter and maintained by what its brochure calls a grassroots foundation. Well, the grass is green indeed in Palo Alto. This is one of very few gardens that have ever made me wish I were wearing a long skirt to stroll it; the layout and contents show what geometry and gentility are *for*. You can call the wedding coordinator,

Gabrielle Gross, at (650) 329-1356, Monday through Friday, 9 A.M. to noon, if you have a particular sort of skirt in mind. The wedding services here are incredibly comprehensive, including rehearsal time, kitchen, decorations, dressing rooms . . . everything but the appropriate principals.

There are scads of more frequently useful services, too: a horticultural reference library (weekdays 9 A.M. to noon); classes, field trips, lectures, and volunteer gardening sessions. The center also hosts the Master Gardeners Program and its services; phone-in questions are answered on Fridays from 1 P.M. to 4 P.M. (650) 329-1356, and a diagnostic clinic is held the second Saturday each month from 9 A.M. to 11 A.M. There are teas, by paid reservation, on the third Wednesday of each month.

SAN MATEO ARBORETUM
Central Park
605 Parkside Way
San Mateo
(650) 579-0536 (San Mateo Arboretum Society)
Wheelchair accessible

This handsome park has something for everyone: picnic space, a playground, a kiddie train, meandering paths, open space, and formal gardens such as a rose garden, a fern grove, and a rhododendron and azalea garden. The rose garden has a gazebo in which weddings are sometimes celebrated. The whole thing is maintained by the San Mateo Arboretum Society, with private donations and volunteer work. These volunteers run a nursery that sells an interesting and varying selection of plants—houseplants, edibles, annuals, and perennials— grown and potted up from seed and from their own gardens. The greenhouses and nursery are open for sales Tuesdays, Thursdays, and Sundays from 10 A.M. to 3 P.M.; prices are low and plants are healthy. (See page 93)

Central Park also includes the City of San Mateo Japanese Garden, which is fenced off separately, open Monday through Friday 10 A.M. to 4 P.M. and weekends 11 A.M. to 4 P.M. Definitely a relaxing stroll, this garden has a few slightly heterodox facets; many of the specimen plants are labeled, for example, and the tea house has recorded music. The koi in the central pond are fed at 11 A.M. and 3 P.M. on weekdays. There are some traditional methods of tree-shaping to be seen here, like bamboo splints and rocks artfully tied and hung as branch weights.

FILOLI
Cañada Road
Woodside
Office Monday–Friday 9 A.M.–2 P.M.
(650) 366-4640
House and garden tours, hikes:
(650) 364-2880
Bookstore and Garden Shop:
Tuesday–Saturday, 10 A.M.–4 P.M. February–November
Excellent bookstore is open and accessible even if you haven't reserved or paid for a tour.
Garden is wheelchair accessible.

This is one of the area's best-endowed public gardens, a legacy of the last century's silver and railroad fortunes. It's formal and expansive, divided into garden rooms by enormous clipped hedges, with everything meticulously mowed and sheared; even the less-formal olive trees in the parking lot have a disciplined air. There are splendid managed views, pools, and fountains; a stained-glass-window flowerbed, no end of extravagant gestures. If your group wants to spend more time and attention on the gardens than in the house, say so; the docents are cheerful about that kink. Filoli has a garden shop and bookstore (see above) and runs nature hikes on the less-cultivated portion of the property near Crystal Springs Reservoir. There are events like concerts, and classes on art and garden subjects; internships are available. Tours need to be arranged, and there's an admission charge; call the office number during open hours.

SOUTH BAY

ENVIRONMENTAL STUDIES AREA
De Anza College
21250 Stevens Creek Boulevard
Cupertino
(408) 864-8346
Open to the public on the first Sunday of each month, 10 A.M.–2 P.M.
Free tours for school groups or the community; contact Doug Cheeseman.
Partly wheelchair accessible; very rough, ungraded paths.

California's flora concentrated into a one-and-one-half-acre plot, cleverly and engagingly designed. Just walking from the desert and chaparral areas to the redwood-shaded stream is a sensuous lesson in climate modification. The area may be open on days other than the designated first Sunday, and Biology Department members are friendly enough; it's worth checking out any time you're in the area. To park in the parking lot—and there's not a lot of other close parking—you'll need eight quarters for the permit machine.

GUADALUPE GARDENS
Guadalupe River Park
West Taylor and Spring Streets
San Jose
Daily 8 A.M.–dusk
Wheelchair accessible

GARDEN CENTER
715 Spring Street
San Jose
(408) 298-7657
Call for hours
Wheelchair accessible

This ambitious project makes sensible use of the Guadalupe River's flood-plain, and will help preserve its productive riparian habitat besides. The rose garden is the third stop on the Taylor and Naglee rose-garden marathon, and it's a goal for the serious rosarian. Its layout is a stunner, with its concentric circles and paths of gray or gold quarry fines. (As much as I love quarry fines, I find them annoying to walk on in sandals; I'm always flipping some abrasive bits between soles and feet. Beware.) The roses are meticulously labeled; there are 5,000 of them, 3,000 antique varieties. Accompanying the roses are several other exemplary gardens: drought-tolerant flowers, a rock garden, and a sort of memorial orchard of fruit trees that graced this valley before the Silicon Age. There's also an honest-to-goodness grassy knoll, built up and upholstered in turf, an inviting place to stretch out and watch jet airliners swoop low to land at the airport, if you're in that sort of mood.

JAPANESE FRIENDSHIP GARDEN
1300 Senter Road
San Jose
(408) 286-3626 or (408) 292-8188
Daily 10 A.M.–sunset
Wheelchair accessible; some slopes are steep. Paths are paved.

Here's another kind of Japanese garden entirely, an example of what you can do with Japanese techniques and ample space. This is a good place to visit several seasons in a year, to study good pruning technique and its use on some nontraditional (for Japan) materials. The garden in general is punctuated with plants like palms and crepe myrtle; the latter's trunks are beautifully exposed and polished-looking. A little hill with patches of red-leaved barberry on its sides and a clump of smoketrees on top makes me smile and think of volcanoes. The garden's situation on two main levels allows it to absorb people peacefully and lends motion to its water features; its paths meander artfully to manipulate views and slow down walkers. The turtle islands in the pond are amusingly literal, and despite the Don't Feed the Koi signs there are pond-chow dispensers so you can have the handsome, shameless pond dwellers splashing and jostling at your feet.

JAPANESE GARDEN AT THE BUDDHIST TEMPLE
640 North Fifth Street
San Jose
(408) 293-9292
Wheelchair accessible

No open hours needed; this is a pocket-sized garden on the street in front of the temple. It's worth a look if you're in San Jose's officially designated Japantown to shop or visit. Once you've passed the prominently displayed memento mori quotation about how we're growing into death all our lives— the Buddhist version of "All Hath Sinned" I guess—there's a compact example of life in the form of koi, pine, juniper, and visiting birds, going cheerfully about its business, even in constrained city circumstances.

OVERFELT BOTANICAL GARDENS
McKee Road and Educational Park Drive
San Jose
(408) 27-PARKS
Daily 10 A.M.–sunset
Wheelchair accessible; parts are hilly.

More a park than an intensively educational botanical garden, this is a place for relaxation and picnics (but no BBQs) and a stroll around some decidedly meandering paths. You can walk through a California native-plant and wildlife area—the wildlife seems to be mostly California ground squirrels, but look for ducks in winter—a palm grove, and the Chinese Cultural Garden, with its monumental marble pavilions and striking black monolith from Taiwan. There are small rose and fragrance gardens, too. You can arrange to take a guided tour, reserve the palm grove or areas of the Chinese Garden for weddings, or send your kids to the Junior Ranger program, which includes tree planting.

What is a garden? There is no consensus yet, and the question's bigger than iit looks. To get a look at its whole shape, step back into the wilderness. That's a longer step than you might think: "wild California" is as much a misconception as the old "wild Indian," and for some of the same reasons. The idea that the Spanish explorers strode into an untouched, untamed land—whatever that means—is a major historical hoax. California's indigenous humans were gardeners, and their gardens were big and various, many days' walk in diameter, and carefully and knowledgeably tended.

Maybe the Europeans were deceived by the fact that indigenes didn't use plows or fences, or domesticate a lot of animals. By all accounts, game and fish were reliably plentiful, a more logical meat source than cattle, and anyone who watched (as I did) the Central Valley dust storm several years ago might think twice about plowing California soils. The absence of these markers customary to Eurasian and African farming didn't mean the landscape wasn't intensely managed, though. We know, for example, that many of the plants of economic importance were planted and replanted where they would thrive, that, for example, the Owens Valley Paiute tilled, irrigated, and crop-rotated their fields. We know that people pruned mesquite and elderberry shrubs to increase their yield and make them more accessible. We know that redbud and buttonwillow were coppiced—pruned hard to encourage long, straight new shoots, or water sprouts—for basket and arrow material. Fern patches were sheared; sedge bogs were worked and loosened, to allow roots to grow unusually long and unkinked. Most of the plants used in baskets must have been managed; compare the stems and rhizomes you see in a big Maidu cooking basket with plants in the wild. No kinks, no bud scars, no knuckles—any of these would make the basket leak. Those watertight museum pieces are the result of biotechnology.

That technology includes the conservation of unique resources, and an obvious knowledge of plant physiology. A good example of both is the use of certain carefully chosen Utah juniper trees (*Juniperus osteosperma*) to make hunting bows. This is trickier than it may sound. First, the bowmaker had to find a straight juniper; many are picturesquely twisted. Good bow wood has to be straight, with no checks or knots, so the tree also had to be an old and healthy one with few branches. The bow should be combined heartwood and sapwood, so it had to come from near the center of the tree. It also had to be kept straight while seasoning for a year or more. The solution to this was elegant: a section of tree ideal for a bow was partially cut away from the living tree, its ends severed from the tree's circulatory system. When this stave was removed later, the tree was left standing: a number are still alive, some with the marks of many uses.

ROSICRUCIAN MUSEUM GARDENS
1342 Naglee Avenue
San Jose
(408) 947-3636
Daily to 9 P.M.
Circuitously wheelchair accessible

You could make this stop two of a San Jose Rose Tour; it's conveniently located between the Civic Rose Garden and Guadalupe River Park. The rose varieties here are not labeled; it's not officially a public resource, after all, and its purposes are somewhat different. Roses, of course, figure in Rosicrucian symbology, and so there are lots of them here, in neat rows and lining walkways, nearly all trained as standards, many with picturesque, gnarly trunks. Things Egyptian have meaning here, too, and so there are big date palms, papyrus, and agapanthus (lily of the Nile), as well as tropical-looking things like banana and monstera, and other species scattered about for reasons I won't pretend to understand if they're not just for looks. In general, this is a relaxing place, if a good example of what happens when a gardener or group of them is seized by a theme; it's also—with its sphinxes, obelisks, Moorish tile fountain, open temple, murals, mosaics, bas-reliefs, and statue of Augustus Caesar—a definitive collection of garden ornaments.

SAN JOSE MUNICIPAL ROSE GARDEN
Naglee Avenue at Garden Drive
San Jose
(408) 277-5561
8 A.M.–dusk
Wheelchair accessible, if you can navigate a lawn.

A formal turf-and-hybrid-tea-rose sort of garden, with its roses laid out in neat quadrangles nestled in grass and punctuated by redwoods, pools, and fountains. They're labeled, which public roses ought to be, and some of them climb and some of them are miniatures and some are just rosy roses. The scent of the place is inspiring enough, and the layout is conducive to ceremony, so the garden is popular for weddings and graduation ceremonies, for which it can be reserved. No wine and roses, though; the garden is subject to the city's park alcohol restrictions.

ORGANICITY

Of course it's all organic; we're talking about carbon-based life forms here. But the word's shorthand meaning—grown without the use of certain so-called synthetic chemicals—is widely understood, and I find it useful. As we see it in markets and nurseries, "organic" is also as much about marketing as about science; to get that California Certified Organic Farm seal, a grower has to jump through hoops that sometimes have little to do with environmental safety, and organic supplements, controls, and other additives can be misused as easily and dangerously as any synthetic chemical. That nice safe sulfur dust that gets rid of mildew on grape leaves and even does the soil some good when it lands there can be disastrous if it gets into a creek in any quantity, becoming, in effect, a megadose of acid rain.

But in my experience, both as a gardener and as what Calvin Trillin calls a Serious Eater, there are good things associated with the label. Locally, CCOF growers have been paying attention to underused fruits and vegetables, both heirloom varieties and interesting new kinds. And while I wouldn't expect that pesticides or fertilizers used on a seedling in the propagator's greenhouse would have health effects on me when I handle or consume the end product, they can affect the bit of the biological world around the greenhouse, and the shipper, and the wholesaler, and the manufacturer, and I like having the chance to make an end run around that.

GARDEN TOURS

Garden tours are getting more and more popular as a fund-raising tool for garden associations, historical societies, schools, and clubs, and new ones start every year. It's a good idea: gardeners get to show off; tourists get to see private gardens that are usually not accessible, and we get to visit public gardens in the company of knowledgeable guides. However difficult it may be, tour manners dictate no touching (let alone filching cuttings) of plants without the gardener's express permission; tour traffic alone can be hard enough on a garden. If something's irresistible, take notes, and consider that you'll probably have better luck if you ask for a bit of plant matter later, when you're not in the company of twenty other similarly lustful onlookers. Some private gardens may not be wheelchair accessible, and participants change from year to year, so ask the sponsor when you call about tickets. Like an informal walk through a public garden, a garden tour is a great source of inspiration and bright ideas, and information isn't hard to get; nothing loosens up a gardener like a wide-eyed, sincere "How did you *do* that?"

BAY AREA IN GENERAL

ANNUAL OPEN GARDEN DAY
San Francisco, East Bay, Marin
Sponsored by Center for Urban Education about Sustainable Agriculture

(510) 526-2788
Early June

A self-guided open-house tour of community gardens, greening projects (including some that are still only proposals), and school and teaching gardens in the Bay Area—most of them in San Francisco and East Bay locations. Map brochures show up in garden-oriented locations, farmers' markets, libraries, and such by May each year, or call the CUESA number for information. (See also the Public Gardens chapter of this book; many of the gardens open this weekend are easily seen from the street and often have people working in them who are happy to talk about what you're seeing.)

EAST BAY

ST. JOSEPH BASILICA'S GARDEN CLUB ANNUAL GARDEN TOUR
Alameda
(510) 814-7152
May

Tour gardens in the dreamland of good soil drainage. About $15, box lunches extra.

BERKELEY GRASSROOTS GREENING TOUR
In collaboration with Open Garden Day

Get the map at the Berkeley Farmers' Markets, or call Partners for Parks' Nancy Carleton at (510) 849-0241 or John Theler-Steere at (510) 849-1969, or the Berkeley Community Gardening Collaborative's Kendall Dunnigan at (510) 883-9096. This map of thirty gardens, daylighted creeks, miniparks, and commons is useful anytime, if you can't fit them all in on the official Open Garden Day. That weekend, of course, has the advantages of produce, plant, and T-shirt sales, children's activities, and talks.

CLAYTON HISTORICAL SOCIETY ANNUAL GARDEN TOUR
Clayton (Contra Costa County)
(510) 672-0240
April

Private gardens of Clayton and the Clayton Museum. About $8.

NILES ART AND WILDFLOWER FESTIVAL GARDEN TOUR
Niles
(510) 742-9868
May

The Niles Art and Wildflower Festival includes a tour of some twenty local gardens, including Niles's historic rose garden. About $5, what a deal.

THE BELLEVUE CLUB
525 Bellevue Avenue
Oakland
(510) 451-1000
Late May

A short tour of some very choice, private Oakland and Piedmont gardens; the tour is pretty private too. Your best bet is to be a member already or go as a guest of someone who is. Benefits the Bellevue Club Heritage Fund.

SECRET GARDENS OF THE EAST BAY
Park Day School Tour
Oakland
(510) 653-6250
April

The justly famous fund-raiser for Park Day School has a different theme—water features, for example—every year, and takes in approximately ten private gardens. About $30, box lunch extra.

HEATHER FARM GARDEN CENTER SPRING GARDEN TOUR

1540 Marchbanks Drive
Walnut Creek
(510) 947-1678
May

Four private gardens in the Walnut Creek—Lafayette area. About $30.

RUTH BANCROFT GARDEN TOUR AND TEA

Walnut Creek
(510) 210-9663
April

Local private gardens, and Ruth Bancroft's own garden; includes food and drink. If you like the public part of the Bancroft Garden, wait till you see the private section. About $20.

NORTH BAY

LARNER SEEDS ANNUAL OPEN HOUSE

235 Grove Road
Bolinas
(415) 868-9407
May

Larner's demonstration garden, a little different every year, is a glorious sight for native-plant lovers.

SONOMA COUNTY FOOD BANK ANNUAL SPRING GARDEN TOUR

Forestville
(707) 887-1647
May

A tour of Sonoma County's private gardens, augmented by an optional high tea. About $25 for tour, $15 for tea.

MILL VALLEY ART AND ARCHITECTURE
Mill Valley
(415) 383-2582
May

Home and garden tour, focuses on both. About $20; box lunch extra.

HIDDEN GARDENS OF OLD TOWN NAPA
Napa
(888) 255-1836 or (707) 255-1836
May

Features gardens in Napa's historic district and light refreshments at the end. Benefits the Napa County Landmarks Association, which also runs a Christmas tour of Victorian homes. About $18.

THROUGH THE GARDEN GATE
Petaluma
(707) 769-0429
May

Nearly a dozen gardens in the Petaluma area. Benefits the Petaluma Historic Library and Museum; about $15.

BEYOND THE GARDEN GATE
Ross
(415) 721-2700 ext. 40
May

This one has included gardens by Topher Delany and other landscapers of note. It benefits the fine arts programs in the Ross public school system. About $25; $15 more for box lunch.

BURBANK GARDEN EXPOSITION
Luther Burbank Garden
Santa Rosa and Sonoma Avenues
Santa Rosa
(707) 524-5445
June

A one-garden tour, but what an historic garden. Burbank's garden isn't big; it's free to walk through during daylight hours, but the house and greenhouse tours are generally scheduled, controlled events. This exposition opens them to self-guided tours, and throws in experts, demonstrations, displays by commercial nurseries, music, and food. Admission about $5; children free.

PENINSULA

SAN MATEO ARBORETUM SOCIETY'S ANNUAL
HILLSBOROUGH GARDEN TOUR
Hillsborough
(650) 344-5350 or (650) 579-0536
May

About five spring gardens and a plant sale, informal lectures, flower arranging instruction, more. Benefits the San Mateo Arboretum. About $20; box lunch available by reservation, about $10.

Ticket reservations: SASE to San Mateo Arboretum Society, 55 Baywood Avenue, San Mateo, CA 94402. Tickets also go on sale at several San Mateo and area commercial nurseries.

ANNUAL GAMBLE SPRING GARDEN TOUR
The Elizabeth F. Gamble Garden Center
1431 Waverley Street
Palo Alto
(650) 329-1356
FAX (650) 329-1688
First Friday and Saturday in May, 10 A.M.–4 P.M.

Self-guided tour of private gardens, plus the gardens at Gamble Garden Center in full spring bloom. Plant clinic by UC master gardeners; sales of garden goods, plants, and seedlings; silent auction; tea and cookies offered throughout the day.

Box lunches are available; reservations required. Call or fax for questions and reservations. Tour fee about $20 to $25.

PESCADERO GARDEN TOUR
Pescadero
(650) 879-9613
Late spring

Private and semi-public gardens on the San Mateo coast. Tour of about six gardens in an area rarely thus exploited. Ever wonder why the food at Duarte's is so good? Check out their produce garden for one reason. Benefits the Pescadero Educational Foundation, which benefits the district's public schools; about $15.

FILOLI TOUR AND MORE
Cañada Road
Woodside
(510) 643-7265
April

Filoli estate and gardens and two private estate gardens, plus lunch. Benefits UC Botanical Garden; cost to nonmembers about $100.

SOUTH BAY

GARDENS OF THE VALLEY OF HEART'S DELIGHT
San Jose
(408) 298-7657
April

A tour of four gardens, sponsored by the Guadalupe Park garden supporters. About $10.

CLASSES AND INFORMATION SOURCES

GENERAL BAY AREA AND INFORMATION SOURCES

BIO-INTEGRAL RESOURCE CENTER
P.O. Box 7414
Berkeley, CA 94707
(510) 524-2567
FAX (510) 524-1758

Two publications, and lots of good advice on Integrated Pest Management and least-toxic methods.

CALIFORNIA OAK FOUNDATION
1212 Broadway, Suite 810
Oakland, CA 94612
(510) 763-0282

Information you may not have known you needed. Native live oaks, for example, are tough and well-adapted to their natural conditions. In a home or public garden, however, they have definite preferences, like not being watered in the dry season, and their roots extend farther than you might think. These folks, or CNPS, can give you what you should know if you have the good fortune to live with a California live oak.

UC AGRICULTURAL COOPERATIVE EXTENSION
Locations throughout the Bay Area; see below.

The extension runs master gardener programs and phone help lines in every county. Master gardener programs train gardeners in all sorts of useful techniques and areas, in return for passing some of that lore on as a community service.

SAN FRANCISCO COUNTY
300 Piedmont Avenue, Room 305A
San Bruno
(650) 871-7559

MARIN COUNTY
1682 Novato Boulevard, Suite 150-B
Novato
(415) 899-8620

ALAMEDA COUNTY
224 West Winton Avenue, Room 174
Hayward
(510) 670-5200

SAN MATEO COUNTY
625 Miramontes Street, Suite 200
Half Moon Bay
(650) 726-9059

CONTRA COSTA COUNTY
1700 Oak Park Boulevard,
Building A-2
Pleasant Hill
(510) 646-6540

SANTA CLARA COUNTY
1005 Timothy Drive
San Jose
(408) 299-2635

SAN FRANCISCO

CITY COLLEGE OF SAN FRANCISCO
Horticulture Department
50 Phelan Avenue
San Francisco
(415) 239-3000

CCSF has a particularly strong floriculture program, with lots of material, greenhouse space, and job referrals. The hort department in general is a good place to learn the elements of garden design, construction, and planting, and there are lively experiments dotted around the grounds, providing examples of raised beds, intensive methods, and the like. A posted help wanted/jobs board makes it a likely place to find some more-skilled-than-average help, too.

CITY COLLEGE OF SAN FRANCISCO CONTINUING EDUCATION
Fort Mason, Building B
Laguna and Marina Boulevard
San Francisco
(415) 561-1860

Some gardening and other classes are held at CCSF's Fort Mason Art Campus.

FRIENDS OF THE URBAN FOREST
San Francisco
(415) 543-5000

Tree walks and tours, and information about street trees, their health, and which ones are good choices. FUF plants, maintains, and educates citizens about trees in San Francisco.

Walk down any street and look at trees. Do you see stubs of obviously amputated limbs? Do you see trees that have been topped—beheaded—maybe to accommodate the utility lines over them? Do you see poodle-shaped shrubs and truffula trees? Now that you're looking, don't they just jump out and yell Uggglly!? That's what Cass Turnbull of Seattle thought, too, and she did something about it. She founded PlantAmnesty. Born of a hypothetical question at a personal development class, PA took on its own life with a referral service and classes, and a slide show of Pruning Horrors as a consciousness-raiser. Now it's spreading beyond Seattle, and sprouts are coming up here.

The principles of good pruning—at least of pretty good pruning—are few and not hard to learn. The principle that PlantAmnesty rides hardest is Never Never Top a Tree. This one gets a lot of abuse in places where views are prized and expensive. A view interrupted or framed by a tree is somehow diminished, and certainly not what a homeowner paid for. So down comes the offending tree—often with the force of local law behind the cutting. So as not to look like clear-cutters, view fetishists will cut just the top several feet, instead of the whole tree; this strategy produces grotesque crew cut cedars, beheaded pines, birches with bad mohawks. It often kills the tree, and slow death is not lovely.

Trees also get topped because they were planted in the wrong place: under utility wires, as I mentioned, or under the eaves or shading the only window on the second floor. The real solution, of course, is forethought: know what you're planting and what it's likely to do. There are small trees and big shrubs that will stop about where you want them to. Those fast-growing Miraculous Purple Princess Majesty Festoon things advertised in the back of *Parade* probably aren't among them. Barring forethought, or the opportunity for forethought, buy a good pruning book; better yet, take a class or sit at the feet of a good arborist, and learn.

People panic and have trees topped because they watch the news and see great big eucalypti falling in a storm, slicing houses in half and squashing the inhabitants like bugs. Then the east-wind moaning in the *Wotsis giganticus* outside takes on a distinct undertone of menace. This fear is not completely irrational, but topping to allay it is. Topping makes a tree *more* dangerous, not less, by evoking masses of wind-catching new growth in the tree. This new wood is ugly; it also makes the tree *more* likely to be blown down. It itself is not so reliably attached to the trunk, and is more likely to fall off and spear some innocent passer-by. One rather ominous piece of literature PlantAmnesty sends to professionals is titled "Are You a Candidate for a Lawsuit?"

PlantAmnesty is a fairly jolly organization, as crusades go; these folks take their vehement rhetoric lightly. PA issues a quarterly newsletter of gardening advice, in-house news, publicity snips, and humor like the Tales of Horror page and pics of entries in the Ugly Yard Contest. The group is a zesty part of the general movement toward the sane handling of trees, public and private. What it advocates is applicable anywhere, and there is some movement toward budding chapters here and in other places. Inquire about it when you contact PA.

PlantAmnesty
906 NW 87th Street
Seattle, WA 98117
(206) 783-9813

SAN FRANCISCO LEAGUE OF URBAN GARDENERS (SLUG)
2088 Oakdale Avenue
San Francisco, CA 94124
(415) 285-7584

SLUG teaches organic and inexpensive gardening methods, composting, and other urban gardening skills. (See page 88.)

STRYBING ARBORETUM SOCIETY
Ninth Avenue and Lincoln Way
Golden Gate Park
San Francisco
(415) 661-1316 ext. 354

Classes, tours, and an excellent bookstore concentrated in an impressively small kiosk—a bonsai'd bookstore. Some lectures are free; most classes cost from $12 to $70 for a single session. (The $70 class in the current catalog includes lunch.) Some class series are $125 to $225: high-end stuff with the likes of Glenn Keator and Ted Kipping. If you join the society, you'll get a quarterly newsletter and calendar, and discounts on classes.

STRYBING ARBORETUM SOCIETY CHILDREN'S EDUCATION
Ninth Avenue and Lincoln Way
San Francisco
(415) 661-1316 ext. 307

Twice-a-month Sunday morning story hours for children, and an interesting series of classes for them, too, in craft and natural-history aspects of gardening.

UC BERKELEY EXTENSION
55 Laguna Street
San Francisco
(510) 642-4111

Many classes are held at UCBE's city center. Classes here tend to be pricey, but they're comprehensive; you can get a degree or certificate in several land-scaping fields. Ask for a catalog.

EAST BAY

ALAMEDA COUNTY
Home Composting Education Program
The Rotline: (510) 635-6275
1933 Davis Street #308
San Leandro, CA 94577

Free classes on worm and regular composting, Saturdays and some evenings. Call for a schedule. Classes are held mostly in these four locations:
LAKESIDE PARK IN OAKLAND (near Garden Center building at Lake Merritt)
TRI-CED RECYCLING CENTER, 33377 Western Avenue, Union City
LIVERMORE COMPOST DEMONSTRATION GARDEN, 3589 Pacific Avenue
   (next to Engineering Building), Livermore
DUBLIN COMPOST DEMONSTRATION GARDEN, Shannon Park, Shannon
   Avenue and San Ramon Road, Dublin

CHERRY BLOSSOM BONSAI STUDIO
1935 Palo Verde Drive
Concord
(510) 685-0454

Ann Gyokurei Nakatani, who taught ikebana at Diablo Valley College for many years, teaches it privately now. She also teaches bonsai, and offers bonsai services like repotting, pruning, and debugging. Call for information and appointment.

DIABLO VALLEY COLLEGE
Horticulture Department
321 Golf Club Road
Pleasant Hill
(510) 685-1230 ext. 443 or ext. 478

DVC's small but effective program will teach you plant materials and how to use them, propagation, pest and disease control by natural means, arboriculture, and, most notably, how plants adapt to their environments, what those environments are like, and how to care for both. Some of these classes are taught by means of field trips led by Stew Winchester, whose sense of ecological and cultural integration in these matters is brilliant. There are adaptive horticulture courses, too, and classes in yardscaping and photographic plant study.

EAST BAY URBAN GARDENERS (EBUG)
1801 Adeline Street, Suite 208
Oakland, CA 94607
Office open Tuesday–Thursday
(510) 549-9159

Free composting classes at 59th Street Community Garden in Oakland, and other classes at various sites.

HEATHER FARM GARDEN CENTER

1540 Marchbanks Drive
Walnut Creek
(510) 947-0571

A number of garden and plant clubs hold classes, demonstrations, and sales here; there's a self-explanatory compost facility too.

THE JEPSON HERBARIUM WEEKEND WORKSHOPS

1001 Valley Life Sciences Building #2465
UC Berkeley
Berkeley, CA 94720-2465
(510) 643-7008

Classes about California's plants and ecosystems assume some degree of botanical knowledge, and cost $100 and up.

MERRITT COLLEGE

Landscape Horticulture Department
12500 Campus Drive
Oakland
(510) 436-2413

Quite the horticultural brain trust, in an open and welcoming atmosphere. There are semester-long courses, and shorter fee classes in subjects likely to interest the home gardener: grasses, orchids, building a fountain. Of particular interest is the Aesthetic Pruning series, Saturday courses with hands-on workshops in pruning trees and shrubs for best looks and health. The Urban Community Gardening class is open entry and exit, repeatable, and free; call Tom Branca at (510) 436-2593 for information. It's held Wednesdays and Saturdays from 9 A.M. to noon. There's also a job referral service for students, making this an excellent source of relatively inexpensive skilled help when you need it.

MILLS COLLEGE
Leadership Institute for Teaching Elementary Science

Coursework for elementary school teachers in Oakland; how to use a worm compost box and/or a school garden for interdisciplinary lessons. They'll give your classroom a worm box, too. If you live in Oakland and want to infect your kids with gardening, ask their teachers to call (510) 834-5342.

UC BOTANICAL GARDEN
200 Centennial Drive
Berkeley
(510) 642-2755
http://www.mip.berkeley.edu/garden/

Classes, garden tours, and a very good small bookstore. There's also a plant clinic on the first Saturday of each month from 9 A.M. to noon. (See page 39.)

NORTH BAY

POINT REYES FIELD SEMINARS
Point Reyes Station
(415) 663-1200

Includes botany and wildflower field classes. Marin spring wildflowers are serious inspiration for gardeners.

SLIDE RANCH
2025 Shoreline Highway
Muir Beach
(415) 381-6155

Family classes in farm and garden practices, as well as in natural history and old skills like spinning and goat-milking.

PENINSULA

CANOPY, TREES FOR PALO ALTO
3921 East Bayshore Road
Palo Alto
(650) 964-6110

Information and tree tours; two-hour course on the hows and whys of tree planting. Planting volunteers get training in tree-planting techniques, which are always handy to know.

COMMON GROUND
(Ecology Action of the Midpeninsula)
2225 El Camino Real
Palo Alto, CA 94306
(650) 328-6752

Inexpensive classes, mostly on food gardening, sometimes on herbs for teas and fragrance, or roses and such. These folks advocate a method called French Intensive, or Biointensive, Gardening, which concentrates on improving soil fertility and raising lots of food in little space. (See listing on page 180.)

ELIZABETH F. GAMBLE GARDEN CENTER
1431 Waverley Street
Palo Alto
(650) 329-1356

Classes, tours, teas, interesting fund-raisers. (See listing on page 50.)

FILOLI
Cañada Road
Woodside
Office is open Monday–Friday 9 A.M.–2 P.M.
(650) 366-4640
House and garden tours, and wildland hikes
(650) 364-2880

Classes, teas, tours, garden shop. This is one of the area's best-endowed public gardens, a legacy of the last century's silver and railroad fortunes. It's formal and expansive, divided into garden rooms by enormous clipped hedges.

FOOTHILL COLLEGE
Ornamental Horticulture Program
12345 El Monte Road
Los Altos Hills
(650) 949-7402

Foothill doesn't offer the array of noncredit fee courses that Merritt in Oakland runs with home gardeners in mind, but it does have evening, daytime, and a few Saturday credit courses. Some offerings of interest to gardeners in general include a short course called Landscape Horticultural Practices, and classes in basic pruning techniques, principles of urban irrigation systems, landscape construction and installation, and design. If you get into the mad-scientist aspect of gardening, you might look into Foothill's micropropagation class.

Integrated Pest Management is pretty uncontroversial, until you start asking about concrete details. Lots of people say they do it, but they mean lots of different things by it. I talked to Michael Baefsky, a genial and enthusiastic practitioner of IPM and an entomologist with the BioIntegral Resource Center in Berkeley. When I asked him what people do wrong about pests in their gardens, one surprising thing he mentioned was pouring potions indiscriminately into garden soils. Mostly, the offending stuff is fertilizer, but even worse are things like the systemic fungicides people "feed" their roses. This is pretty broad-spectrum, and can sterilize all fungi out of the soil, which is a problem because fungi comprise much of a soil's microbial life; they're most of what keeps it and us alive. "This," said Baefsky, "is degrading the microbial life in soils at the home garden level. Junk is poured into the soil based on myth. Both organic and nonorganic gardeners have myths; organic gardeners' myths are just more sophisticated."

A lot of what passes for garden hygiene—raking the dirt bare, non-selective spraying (including relatively benign horticultural oils), and any sort of broad-target drenching or tilling-in—has the effect of returning the ground and plants to a fairly sterile state every time it's done. As anyone who's taken antibiotics knows, this invites all sorts of grief.

When I asked what IPM ideas work here in the Bay Area, Baefsky mentioned biodegradable black Hortpaper, available from Peaceful Valley Farm Supply (see below), for weed control. A more commercial weed control technique being tested on Alameda County roadsides and organic cotton farms is a hot-water spray applied to sprouting weeds. Some bright ideas are being refined: Baefsky reported good results against rose and viburnum aphids from releasing large, advanced instars (larval stages) of green lacewing.

Refinements depend on further use and evaluation. Locally, blue stickytraps don't work well to control or monitor thrips, and codling moth traps remain at least unproved. For the latter, Baefsky recommends sanitation and banding and tolerating some damage. (You band the tree, not the moth.) Ill-timed or sloppy spraying can wipe out the mites that are codling moths' chief predators. Another spray horror Baefsky mentioned is routine annual treatment for oakmoths; he prefers to count the worms and the frass under the trees to see when spraying is necessary. What he does do routinely is tell clients to stop watering live oaks; this helps keep them healthy enough to shrug off the moths, which have coexisted with them just fine, thank you, for longer than we have. Live oaks are among California's most biologically productive plants, with lots of organisms depending on them in one way or another.

Peaceful Valley Farm Supply takes mail and phone orders, or you can see their store in person at 110 Spring Hill Boulevard in Grass Valley. Their catalog costs $2. Call them at (530) 272-4769, or write to P.O. Box 2209, Grass Valley, CA 95945.

SOUTH BAY

EMMA PRUSCH PARK
647 South King Road
San Jose
(408) 299-4147

Master composters teach composting basics once a month on Saturday from 9 A.M. to 11 A.M. Free. There are additional classes for adults and children, too, and a kids' summer farm camp.

ONLINE RESOURCES

THE BAY AREA GARDENER WEB SITE

This one is primo. Informative, useful, just idiosyncratic enough to be personable, this one is high on my bookmark list. Lots of links to other gardening sites, but this might be the only one you need. **http://www.gardens.com**

CALIFORNIA NATIVE PLANT SOCIETY WEB SITE

Informative, scholarly, comprehensive; it even has a kids' section.
http://www.calpoly.edu/~dchippin/cnps_main.html

MEDITERRANEAN PLANTS MAILING LIST

Mediterranean plants, of course, are the sort that thrive in the kind of climate we have here, as well as around the Mediterranean, in Chile, in parts of Australia, and around the southern tip of Africa. To join, email **sean.ohara@ucop.edu.**

A number of rose societies have Web sites, with providers of varying reliability. The easiest thing I've found is to go the Bay Area Gardener site, or to the American Rose Society site, at **http://www.ars.org** and link from there.

GARDENING NEWSGROUPS

I find **rec.gardens.edible** fairly useful. The amount of information posted there has been known to vary a lot, depending on the status of associated mailing lists and on participants' inclinations.

So general as to be almost irrelevant, **rec.arts.gardens** covers gardens everywhere, and conditions here are very dissimilar from those, say, back East. Like a lot of large newsgroups, it's diluted by generalization.

The interplay among levels of skill, experience, and fanaticism makes **rec.arts.bonsai** interesting, if you work on or follow bonsai.

There's a rose fanciers' newsgroup, too: **rec.gardens.roses.**

The usefulness and fun of any newsgroup will ebb and flow over time. Remember, newsgroups are not a spectator sport. If there's one you wish were livelier, go on in and stir up the pot. Asking an interesting question is a much better way to do this than starting or joining an argument; fights generally drive away more knowledgeable people than they attract.

OTHER CIVIC RESOURCES

Alameda County residents can get a Biostack composter, one per household, for under $40; at retail it would cost upwards of $80. I have one, and can guarantee that it works even if you don't compost according to the rubrics. There's also a less-elaborate open hoop composter available for about half the cost. **Call the Rotline (510) 635-6275.**

San Mateo County residents have a similar deal, a Biostack for $35, also one per household. **Call (650) 363-4100.**

The Alameda County Mosquito Abatement District will give county residents free mosquito-eating gambusia fish for their ponds or water gardens. **Call (510) 783-7744.** They'll deliver.

Berkeley residents can borrow tools from the Tool Library: ladders, pruners, goggles, shovels, picks, even house jacks. You'll need to show an ID with a Berkeley address, and sign a waiver.

BERKELEY PUBLIC LIBRARY
Tool Library
1901 Russell Street
Berkeley
(510) 644-6101
Wheelchair accessible

RESTORATION AND COMMUNITY GARDENS

Working with restoration gardeners is a good way to get educated in ecological issues, local soils, native-plant gardening, and efficient methods for
any garden. Community gardens give members a bit of dirt to use, and,
more important, community. The information you get there, and the neigh-
borly exchange, can be as energizing as the fresh produce you grow—and
trade for.

BAY AREA ACTION
(650) 321-1994

Working to restore Montara Mountain and more. This organization has a
spirited and engaging way of going about its good work. For example, its
way to promote sustainable agriculture and low-impact eating is to throw
parties and feasts. I like this group's attitude.

CNPS NATIVE PLANT PROPAGATION
Merritt College
Landscape Horticulture Department
12500 Campus Drive
Oakland
(510) 559-9269 or (510) 376-4095

The California Native Plant Society, East Bay Chapter, holds a potting and grooming party every Tuesday from 9 A.M. to 2 P.M. It's useful—plants are for CNPS's October benefit sale—hands-on educational, and fun. Bring clippers, gloves, two quarters for parking, and lunch.

COMMUNITY ORGANIC GARDENING
Bay Area Action
(650) 321-1994

Work parties in midtown Palo Alto behind Baskin-Robbins, on Sundays from 10 A.M. to 2 P.M.

EAST PALO ALTO COMMUNITY GARDEN
831 Weeks Street
(650) 852-9629

Bay Area Action and the East Palo Alto Historical and Agricultural Society sponsor work sessions on Saturdays from 9 A.M. to noon.

SAVE MOUNT DIABLO
P.O. Box 5376
Walnut Creek, CA 94596
(510) 229-4275 or (510) 549-0211

A native meadow restoration is in progress on the mountain. You could learn how to drive a tractor or mower, or you can just plant lots and lots of seedlings and learn more than you thought there was to know about native California bunchgrasses and the wildflowers and critters they shelter.

URBAN CREEKS COUNCIL
1250 Addison Street, Suite 107C
Berkeley, CA 94704
(510) 540-6669

This group engages in daylighting creeks, restoring their banks and corridors to a more natural state, and educating people about how to keep their local watersheds healthy. You can learn about native flora and fauna, applied small-space engineering, and even hydraulics.

KARL LINN

Karl Linn, who has a community garden in north Berkeley named for him, is one of EBUG's "seedpeople." I asked him what had brought him to value community gardens, and why he works for EBUG. By way of an answer, he told me his life story.

Born in prewar Germany, Linn grew up in the only Jewish family in a village of about five hundred. When he was eight or ten years old, his playmates tried to include him in their social group, the local Hitlerjugend troop, until, as he says, "they realized I was their only opportunity for target practice." By age fourteen, he'd dropped out of school and put himself to work raising his family's food in his mother's garden. When his family emigrated to Palestine, he lived on a kibbutz and absorbed ideals of community there. When he learned Arabic, and started to comprehend more of the dialogue among his neighbors, he noticed that "the community didn't extend to the Arabs" in Israel. This, he said, seemed entirely too familiar.

After he'd emigrated again, to the United States, he found one field of study leading to another: Gestalt psychology to horticultural therapy to landscape architecture, which is applied psychology on a grand scale. His life had given him a respect and thirst for community, and he's been working to foster it in various ways since boyhood.

Linn sees his work as a counter-force to the enclosure of the commons, the dividing and privatizing tendency that's been at work in Western society since the time of the English Diggers and Cromwell and the Black-and-Tans. (Remember the root causes of the Irish Potato Famine?) He draws the analogy to barn raising, in which community interdependence strengthens community independence. And he prizes the urban commons, where people are, he says, "in each other's presence, not in each other's way."

SLUG and EBUG

For the last few decades, weedy lots in midcity have one by one been coaxed to yield bounty and beauty by determined and imaginative community gardeners. Some have been turned around by city people hungry to garden something, somewhere; some have been part of organized clean-up campaigns; some have been do-gooder projects by college classes. Some are temporary, some have become institutions. All have blessed the ground and the neighborhood with good things to eat and look at, good places to be. They bring isolated people together as a community and foster the good things that rise from that. They're one of the city's best ideas.

Something more has happened in San Francisco and again in the East Bay. Some sort of critical mass has been reached, and scattered gardens are coming together to form an even more useful whole: urban garden leagues. The San Francisco League of Urban Gardeners (SLUG) and the East Bay Urban Gardeners (EBUG) are cooperating relatives, a network that includes local colleges and universities, school districts, nurseries, homegrown experts, first-time diggers, guerrilla gardeners, artistes and politicos, parents, kids, small businesses, civic leaders, and all sorts of plant-lovers. What they're doing is the next step in urban and community gardening.

SAN FRANCISCO LEAGUE OF URBAN GARDENERS (SLUG)
2088 Oakdale Avenue
San Francisco, CA 94124
(415) 285-7584

SLUG coordinates community garden starts in San Francisco; it gets gardens up and running and self-managed by the gardeners who use them. SLUG's demonstration garden, the Garden for the Environment, is at Seventh Avenue and Lawton in San Francisco.

SLUG offers memberships at $25 (or sliding scale) a year; membership gets you discounts on SLUG's soil testing service and on its educational events, a 10 percent discount on goods at some twenty area garden stores, and free soil amendments—compost, manure, mulch material—from SLUG's supply yard.

EAST BAY URBAN GARDENERS (EBUG)
1801 Adeline Street, Suite 208
Oakland, CA 94607
Office open Tuesday–Thursday
(510) 549-9159

Ask about openings in your local community garden, or how to set up a new one. EBUG is a few years younger than San Francisco's SLUG and is modeled on that organization; it doesn't yet have as many resources, but is adding new ones all the time, and can also point you toward other sources. Membership in EBUG gives you discounts at supporting nurseries and on EBUG workshop fees and soil tests, access to its tool lending library, a newsletter, and the chance to learn about gardening and community organizing as a volunteer in its projects. EBUG supports gardening and greening projects by training garden organizers; lending design and construction expertise and help; supporting, organizing, and facilitating meetings; sponsoring workdays; donating materials; and providing horticulture employment training, information, and referral; and running classes and workshops. It has also published two handbooks, *Steps to Creating a Community Garden* and *Community Garden Coordinator's Manual*. EBUG-associated Spiral Gardens has been particularly assertive in turning abandoned patches into locally run community gardens.

PLANT AND GARDEN SOCIETIES

You don't have to be a fanatic for a certain sort of plant to join its patron society, but enthusiasm can be contagious. A visit or two to a society meeting can be a good way to educate yourself about something you're fond of, or have just been handed Auntie Ev's collection of, or that caught your eye on a tour. As you can see here, the scope of plant societies is broad, from little bitty houseplants to instant forests to whole ecosystems. Many of the reference phone numbers listed here are for the home phones of club members; please keep this in mind if you call. Also, the offices these folks hold may rotate, so there's a chance of getting referred to this semester's majority whip, or secretary. Don't worry; a sincerely shared interest is a good social lubricant.

Plant club dues are usually fairly low; "Friends of" groups, arboretum societies, and groups big enough to have many chapters generally have levels of membership that start around $20 a year and rise, often with a concomitant rise in benefits and privileges.

Club meetings generally feature talks and problem-solving, news about new varieties, techniques, general information-sharing, and the sale or exchange of seeds, cuttings, sprouts, or plants.

GENERAL SOCIETIES

CALIFORNIA HORTICULTURAL SOCIETY

California Academy of Sciences
Golden Gate Park
San Francisco
(415) 566-5222
Meets third Monday of each month, except December.

This organization publishes *Pacific Horticulture* magazine, which is practically indispensable for serious California gardeners. Meetings include plant sales, talks, slide shows, new plants, botanical adventures, bright ideas.

STRYBING ARBORETUM SOCIETY

Ninth Avenue at Lincoln Way
Golden Gate Park
San Francisco
Office open Monday–Friday, 9:00 A.M.–4:30 P.M.
(415) 661-1316 ext. 301
FAX (415) 661-7427
Email: bphcrl@ix.netcom.com

Joining this support organization gets you a chance to preview its annual plant sale; free admission to several other botanic gardens (Strybing is free to all); 10 percent discounts on programs, books, and plants at Strybing and at supporting nurseries, and a quarterly newsletter, for $35 per year and up.

FRIENDS OF THE REGIONAL PARKS BOTANIC GARDEN

Tilden Regional Park
Berkeley
Membership: (510) 841-8732

Membership starts at $20 a year and gets you a quarterly newsletter, the botanic garden's annual publication *Four Seasons*, and discounts at several nurseries that are good native-plant sources. The garden, in Berkeley's Tilden

Park, is devoted entirely to California natives and, as a genetic treasury and living education, is worth the concerted efforts that have gone into preserving it. Board meetings are generally held the first Thursday of the month at 1 P.M. in the garden; call first to verify the time.

UC BOTANICAL GARDEN
200 Centennial Drive
Berkeley
(510) 642-3343
http://www.mip.berkeley.edu/garden/

Members of the garden get free admission to this and other botanical gardens, previews of plant sales, and discounts on plants and on garden workshops. Workshop subjects include propagation, dried-flower wreaths, local plant communities, and edibles. The organization includes docents and other volunteers. Dues start at $35 annually.

THE MARSHALL OLBRICH PLANT CLUB
Community Room of Glendale Federal Savings
McKinley Street
P.O. Box 1338
Sebastopol, CA 95473
(707) 829-9189

Meets 7:30 P.M., on the third Wednesday of every other month, starting with January. Call or write for information. A general-interest garden club. Anything with Marshall Olbrich's name on it ought to be good.

SAN MATEO ARBORETUM SOCIETY
101 Ninth Avenue
San Mateo, CA 94401
(650) 579-0536

Lots of opportunity for volunteer work and learning. This organization keeps the San Mateo Arboretum going with work and fund-raising, including plant sales every Tuesday, Thursday, and Sunday from 10 A.M. to 3 P.M. It publishes a newsletter and sponsors educational programs, garden workshops, holiday events, tours of members' gardens, an annual garden party, an annual membership dinner, and the Hillsborough Garden Tour. Call or write for information.

WESTERN HORTICULTURAL SOCIETY
Loyola School
Los Altos
(650) 941-1332
Meets second Wednesday of each month at 7:30 P.M.

SOCIETIES FOR SPECIFIC INTERESTS

BAY AREA—WIDE

AMERICAN BAMBOO SOCIETY, NORTHERN CALIFORNIA CHAPTER

Get help in acquiring, growing, and using one of the earth's most versatile plants, even if you're not raising pandas.

David King
480 West "I" Street
Benicia, CA 94510
For membership information, email:
michael-bartholomew@cce.cornell.edu
or write to him at:
750 Krumkill Road
Albany, NY 12203-5976

For the Bamboo Society's Annual Source List, send an SASE to:
Richard Haubrich
P.O. Box 640
Springville, CA 93265

BAY AREA CARNIVOROUS PLANT SOCIETY
39011 Applegate Terrace
Fremont, CA 94537
Membership: (510) 796-9654
http://spiderweb.com/carnivore

Meeting sites vary, from places in Santa Rosa to San Jose. Call or write for information. Meetings feature speakers, cultural tips, and plant sales by members.

GOLDEN GATE CYMBIDIUM SOCIETY
Lakeside Garden Center
666 Bellevue Avenue
Oakland
(510) 276-8067
Wheelchair accessible
Meets fourth Wednesday of each month at 7:30 P.M.

GOLDEN STATE LILY SOCIETY
Lakeside Garden Center
666 Bellevue Avenue
Oakland
(510) 653-7718
Wheelchair accessible
Meeting dates vary.

FRIENDS OF ORCHIDMANIA
OrchidMania
P.O. Box 14666
San Francisco, CA 94114
(415) 558-8444
FAX (415) 558-9180
Email: info@orchids.org

Membership is automatic after a financial gift of $50 or more, a plant donation valued at $100 or more, or spending $300 or more at any of OrchidMania's sales. It gets you early entrance to OrchidMania's orchid sales, invitations to a monthly open house at its greenhouse, classes, and workshops for Friends only, and discounts from commercial orchid growers.

INTERNATIONAL PALM SOCIETY, NORTHERN CALIFORNIA CHAPTER
(415) 681-1855

Quarterly meetings, various Bay Area locations. Did you know you can grow coconuts outdoors in the Bay Area?

CALIFORNIA RARE FRUIT GROWERS, GOLDEN GATE CHAPTER

Meets second Saturday of January, March, May, July, September, and November, at various locations in San Francisco, Alameda, and Contra Costa Counties.
Local contact: (510) 654-6001
With general questions, email:
info@crfg.org
or write to:
California Rare Fruit Growers
The Fullerton Arboretum – CSUF
P.O. Box 6850
Fullerton, CA 92834-6850

OR

Robert Vieth, President
California Rare Fruit Growers
1407 Ellsworth Circle
Thousand Oaks, CA 91360

For membership/subscription questions, contact:
Sue Irvine, CRFG Administrative Assistant
9872 Aldgate Avenue
Garden Grove, CA 92641
(714) 638-1796

CRFG members share information; exchange seeds, plants, and scion wood; give garden tours; exhibit displays and staff information booths at fairs and shows; hold plant sales; and give classes on propagation, pruning, and grafting for members. The state convention, and many chapter meetings, feature speakers who are experts in rare fruit culture; local chapter meetings include plant auctions, freebies, tastings, and sales. Meetings and activities are open to the public as well as members.

CRFG offers a seed-bank service, expert advice, and a book service statewide.

AMERICAN RHODODENDRON SOCIETY
(408) 429-5027
Meetings are held alternately at
Aptos Library
7695 Soquel Drive
Aptos
Wheelchair accessible
AND
UCSC Arboretum
1156 High Street
Santa Cruz
Wheelchair accessible

Meets third Tuesday of each month, except July and August, at 7:30 P.M.

NORTH AMERICAN ROCK GARDEN SOCIETY, WESTERN CHAPTER
2699 Shasta Road
Berkeley, CA 94618
(510) 644-1656

Meets six to eight times a year; the site varies. Getting to see members' alpine gardens is reason enough to join. Call or write for information.

GOLDEN GATE ROSE SOCIETY

San Francisco County Fair Building (Hall of Flowers)
Golden Gate Park
Ninth Avenue at Lincoln Way
San Francisco
(415) 665-5132
Wheelchair accessible
Meets fourth Wednesday of each month at 7:30 P.M.

HERITAGE ROSES GROUP, BAY AREA CHAPTER

100 Bear Oaks Drive
Martinez, CA 94553
(510) 254-0319

Meets twice a year, in spring and fall; the site varies. These folks put on an interesting show and sale in spring (see the Local Sales and Events chapter). Call or write for information.

SAN FRANCISCO

AFRICAN VIOLET SOCIETY OF SAN FRANCISCO

San Francisco County Fair Building (Hall of Flowers)
Golden Gate Park
Ninth Avenue at Lincoln Way
San Francisco
(415) 751-6037
Wheelchair accessible
Meets third Wednesday of each month at 7:30 P.M.

Culture tips, plant swapping, instruction, demonstrations.

SAN FRANCISCO AMERICAN BEGONIA SOCIETY

San Francisco County Fair Building (Hall of Flowers)
Golden Gate Park
Ninth Avenue at Lincoln Way
San Francisco
(415) 931-4912

Wheelchair accessible
Meets first Wednesday of each month at 8 P.M.

CACTUS AND SUCCULENT SOCIETY, SAN FRANCISCO CHAPTER
Strybing Arboretum
Ninth Avenue at Lincoln Way
San Francisco
(650) 359-1220
Wheelchair accessible
Meets third Tuesday of each month at 7:30 P.M.

DAHLIA SOCIETY OF CALIFORNIA
San Francisco County Fair Building (Hall of Flowers)
Golden Gate Park
Ninth Avenue at Lincoln Way
San Francisco
(415) 388-1671
Wheelchair accessible
Meets second Tuesday of each month at 8 P.M.

AMERICAN FUCHSIA SOCIETY, SAN FRANCISCO BRANCH
San Francisco County Fair Building (Hall of Flowers)
Golden Gate Park
Ninth Avenue at Lincoln Way
San Francisco
(415) 664-0917
Wheelchair accessible
Meets first Monday of each month at 7 P.M.

SAN FRANCISCO GESNERIAD AND GLOXINIA SOCIETY
San Francisco County Fair Building (Hall of Flowers)
Golden Gate Park
Ninth Avenue at Lincoln Way
San Francisco
(650) 363-0626

Wheelchair accessible
Meet third Sunday of each month at 1 P.M.

MYCOLOGICAL SOCIETY OF SAN FRANCISCO
Randall Museum
P.O. Box 882163
San Francisco
(415) 759-0495
Meets third Tuesday of each month at 7 P.M., May through October.

There are times when our climate seems to be ideal for raising mushrooms, and mushrooms the ideal crop for the area. As knowledge of spore-raising, inoculation, myceliae, and growing media becomes more sophisticated, reliable, and widespread, mushrooms are becoming a more usual garden crop. There's also a focus on wild mushrooms, of course, and these folks get to eat what they catch.

CALIFORNIA NATIVE PLANT SOCIETY, SAN FRANCISCO (YERBA BUENA) CHAPTER
San Francisco County Fair Building (Hall of Flowers)
Golden Gate Park
Ninth Avenue at Lincoln Way
San Francisco
(415) 731-3028
Wheelchair accessible
Meets fourth Wednesday of each month at 7:30 P.M.

This chapter is involved in restoration and preservation work, which is appropriate since it's based in the territory of the last known Presidio manzanita.

SAN FRANCISCO ORCHID SOCIETY
San Francisco County Fair Building (Hall of Flowers)
Golden Gate Park
Ninth Avenue at Lincoln Way
San Francisco
(415) 665-2468

Wheelchair accessible
Meets first Tuesday of each month at 7:30 P.M.

SAN FRANCISCO ROSE SOCIETY

San Francisco County Fair Building (Hall of Flowers)
Golden Gate Park
Ninth Avenue at Lincoln Way
San Francisco
(415) 436-0497
To see the San Francisco Rose Society Web site, the most reliable route is via
its link with the American Rose Society Web site at http://www.ars.org/.
Wheelchair accessible
Meets second Sunday of each month: workshop at noon; meeting, 1 P.M.

EAST BAY

AFRICAN VIOLET SOCIETY OF DIABLO VALLEY

Heather Farm Garden Center
1540 Marchbanks Drive
Walnut Creek
(415) 751-6037
Wheelchair accessible
Meets first Wednesday of each month at 7:30 P.M.

Culture tips, plant swapping, instruction, demonstrations.

CACTUS AND SUCCULENT SOCIETY, OAKLAND CHAPTER

Lakeside Garden Center
666 Bellevue Avenue
Oakland
Michael Gaddis, newsletter editor: (415) 491-1840
Wheelchair accessible
Meets second Sunday of each month at 1 P.M.

Lore, tips, gossip, and education (is there a difference?) about some of the world's
oddest plants.

DAHLIA SOCIETY OF SAN LEANDRO

San Leandro Library
Estudillo Way
San Leandro
(510) 276-0530
Wheelchair accessible
Meets third Thursday of each month at 7:30 P.M.

EAST BAY FUCHSIA SOCIETY

Northbrae Community Church
941 The Alameda
Berkeley
(510) 527-5889
Wheelchair accessible
Meets third Tuesday of each month at 7:15 P.M.

EDEN FUCHSIA SOCIETY

Calvary Temple
2305 Washington Avenue
San Leandro
(510) 351-1733
Meets second Monday of each month at 11:30 A.M.

RICHMOND FUCHSIA SOCIETY

2434 Colusa Street
Pinole
(510) 758-9519
Meets third Saturday of each month at 2 P.M. Call for information.

SOUTHLANDERS FUCHSIA SOCIETY

Ashland Community Center
1530 167th Avenue
San Leandro
(510) 783-9542
Meets fourth Thursday of each month at 7:30 P.M. except June and July.

FRIENDS OF HEIRLOOM FLOWERS
Niles Rose Garden
Shinn House
1251 Peralta Boulevard
Niles
(510) 656-7702
Work parties Tuesdays and Thursdays.

MOUNT DIABLO IRIS SOCIETY
Heather Farm Garden Center
Walnut Creek
(510) 937-2951
Wheelchair accessible
Meets second Friday of each month at 7:30 P.M.

SYDNEY B. MITCHELL IRIS SOCIETY
Lakeside Garden Center
666 Bellevue Avenue
Oakland
(510) 843-3828
Wheelchair accessible
Meets fourth Friday of each month at 7:30 P.M., February through October.

CALIFORNIA NATIVE PLANT SOCIETY, EAST BAY CHAPTER
P. O. Box 5579
Berkeley, CA 94705
(510) 464-4977
Meets third Wednesday of each month at 7:30 P.M.; location varies.

This is the foundation chapter of CNPS, and it works closely with Tilden Park's native-plant Botanic Garden—in fact, it arose out of the successful effort to save the garden in the 1960s. The chapter's newsletter, the *Bay Leaf*, is informative about plants, talks, chapter field trips, and legislative events concerning conservation. Call or write for information, or ask at a CNPS sale or at the Wildflower Show every spring at the Oakland Museum of California.

DIABLO VIEW ORCHID SOCIETY
Contra Costa Water District headquarters
1331 Concord Avenue
Concord
(510) 685-8904
Meets second Thursday of each month at 7:30 P.M.

ORCHID SOCIETY OF CALIFORNIA
Lakeside Garden Center
666 Bellevue Avenue
Oakland
(510) 839-9647 (ask for Ray Vickers)
Wheelchair accessible
Meets third Monday of each month at 8 P.M.

CONTRA COSTA ROSE SOCIETY
Heather Farm Garden Center
1540 Marchbanks Drive
Walnut Creek
(510) 671-2700 or (510) 376-4325
Wheelchair accessible
Meets fourth Wednesday of each month at 7:30 P.M.

EAST BAY ROSE SOCIETY
Lakeside Park
666 Bellevue Avenue
Oakland
(510) 893-6020
http://www.geocities.com/RainForest/4756
Wheelchair accessible
Meets third Wednesday of each month at 7:30 P.M.

MOUNT DIABLO ROSE SOCIETY
Pleasanton Senior Center
Kottinger Road
Pleasanton
(510) 447-4508
Wheelchair accessible
Meets second Wednesday of each month at 7:30 P.M.

NORTH BAY

CHRYSANTHEMUM SOCIETY OF MARIN
First Baptist Church Meeting Hall
1411 Lincoln Avenue
San Rafael
(415) 472-0160
Meets second Monday of each month at 8 P.M.

SANTA ROSA FUCHSIA SOCIETY
Luther Burbank Art and Garden Center
2050 Yulupa Avenue
Santa Rosa
(707) 545-4950
Meets first Friday of each month at 11:30 A.M.

VALLEJO FUCHSIA SOCIETY
Church of the Ascension
2420 Tuolumne Street
Vallejo
(707) 644-0839
Meets third Tuesday of each month at 7:30 P.M.

CALIFORNIA NATIVE PLANT SOCIETY, MILO BAKER (SONOMA) CHAPTER
Luther Burbank Art and Garden Center
2050 Yulupa Avenue

Santa Rosa
(707) 833-2856
Meets third Tuesday of each month at 7:30 P.M.

This chapter does some interesting work, including a good native-plant sale in October, field trips, weekly Monday plant walks, and a taxonomy workshop at Santa Rosa Junior College. Membership benefits include the chapter newsletter and the excellent quarterly *Fremontia*.

MARIN ORCHID SOCIETY
Marin Art and Garden Center
Sir Francis Drake Boulevard
Ross
(415) 388-4823
Wheelchair accessible
Meets third Thursday of each month at 7:45 P.M.

MARIN ROSE SOCIETY
Marin Art and Garden Center, Livermore Room
Sir Francis Drake Boulevard
Ross
Wheelchair accessible
http://www.hooked.net/~ttrimble/marinrose
Meets second Tuesday of each month at 7:30 P.M., except December.

NORTH BAY ROSE SOCIETY
Florence Douglas Senior Center
333 Amador Street
Vallejo
(707) 746-1542
Wheelchair accessible
Meets second Monday of each month at 7:30 P.M., except September and December.

REDWOOD EMPIRE ROSE SOCIETY
Luther Burbank Art and Garden Center
2050 Yulupa Avenue
Santa Rosa
(707) 579-4663
Meets third Thursday of each month at 7:30 P.M.

PENINSULA

AFRICAN VIOLET SOCIETY OF SAN MATEO COUNTY
San Mateo Garden Center
605 Parkside Way
San Mateo
(650) 593-2998
Wheelchair accessible
Meets second Monday of each month: workshop at 7 P.M.; meeting, 7:45 P.M.

Ideas and techniques for culture of African violets, material exchange, other information.

CACTUS AND SUCCULENT SOCIETY, PENINSULA CHAPTER
San Mateo Garden Center
605 Parkside Way
San Mateo
(650) 592-3366
Wheelchair accessible
Meets second Wednesday of each month at 12:30 P.M., September through June.

FUCHSIA SOCIETY OF PACIFICA
American Legion Hall
555 Buel Street
Pacifica
(650) 359-1227
Meets third Friday of each month at 7:30 P.M.

SAN BRUNO FUCHSIA SOCIETY
San Francisco County Fair Building (Hall of Flowers)
Golden Gate Park
Ninth Avenue at Lincoln Way
San Francisco
(650) 591-9752
Wheelchair accessible
Meets second Monday of each month at 8 P.M.

SAN MATEO COUNTY FUCHSIA SOCIETY
San Mateo Garden Center
605 Parkside Way
San Mateo
(650) 593-8368
Wheelchair accessible
Meets second Tuesday of each month at 7:30 P.M.

PENINSULA GESNERIAD SOCIETY
Palo Alto
(650) 363-0626
Meets first Thursday of each month at 7:30 P.M.; location varies.
Call for information.

WEST BAY IRIS SOCIETY
Garden House
400 University Avenue
Los Altos
(650) 948-4809
Meets third Friday of each month; call for time.

PENINSULA ORCHID SOCIETY
San Mateo Garden Center
605 Parkside Way
(650) 591-0364
Wheelchair accessible

Meets fourth Friday of each month at 8 P.M.

PENINSULA ROSE SOCIETY
Veterans' Memorial Building
1455 Madison Avenue
Redwood City
Email: spitbite@msn.com
Meets second Wednesday of each month at 7:30 P.M.

SOUTH BAY

SOUTH BAY AFRICAN VIOLET SOCIETY
Sunnyview Lutheran Home
22449 Cupertino Road
Cupertino
(408) 736-3803
Wheelchair accessible
Meets third Tuesday of each month at 12:30 P.M.

BEGONIA SOCIETY OF SANTA CLARA VALLEY
Kirk Community Center, Room 2
1601 Foxworthy Avenue
San Jose
(650) 688-0351
Meets third Thursday of each month at 7:45 P.M.

CACTUS AND SUCCULENT SOCIETY, SAN JOSE CHAPTER
Emma Prusch Farms Park
647 South King Road
San Jose
(510) 651-8649
Meets first Sunday of each month at 1 P.M.

Exchange knowledge and materials about these strange and engaging plant groups in a region that seems to be full of people with a fondness for them.

CAMELLIA SOCIETY OF SANTA CLARA COUNTY

Lick Mill Park
4750 Lick Mill Boulevard
Santa Clara
(408) 295-8068
Meets third Wednesday of each month at 7:30 P.M., October through March.

JOHN E. STOWELL DAHLIA SOCIETY

Guadalupe Garden Center
715 Spring Street (at Taylor)
San Jose
(408) 259-9223
Meets fourth Tuesday of each month at 7:30 P.M.

FUCHSIA SOCIETY OF SAN JOSE

St. Edward's Episcopal Church
15040 Union (at Brenham)
San Jose
(408) 257-0752
Meets third Monday of each month at 8 P.M.

FUCHSIA SOCIETY OF SANTA CLARA VALLEY

Hillview Community Center
Hillview Avenue (off San Antonio)
(650) 856-9476
Meets first Tuesday of each month at 7:30 P.M.

CLARA B. REES IRIS SOCIETY

First Baptist Church
17765 Davies Avenue
Los Gatos
(408) 251-3740
Meets first Friday of each month at 7:30 P.M.

JAPANESE BAMBOO SOCIETY OF SARATOGA

Hakone Gardens
2100 Big Basin Way
Saratoga
(408) 264-7024
Meets last Saturday of each month at 10 A.M.

This small group focuses on Asian bamboo varieties, specifically on the ones in Hakone Gardens' Bamboo Park. There are two yearly parties, a sporadic newsletter, and events and programs in association with the Hakone Foundation.

CALIFORNIA NATIVE PLANT SOCIETY, SANTA CLARA CHAPTER

(415) 493-4595
Meets fourth Friday of each month at 7:30 P.M.; call for location.

CNPS engages in education, lobbying, the preservation of rare plants and their habitat. Membership gets you local benefits plus a subscription to *Fremontia*, a scholarly and accessible quarterly.

MALIHINA ORCHID SOCIETY

Oak Room at Hewlett Packard
Prune Ridge
Santa Clara
(408) 262-5782
Meets second Friday of each month at 7:30 P.M.

ORCHID SOCIETY, SANTA CLARA VALLEY CHAPTER

American Legion Hall
1504 Minnesota Avenue
San Jose
(408) 996-8335
Meets first Wednesday of each month at 7:30 P.M.

SANTA CLARA ROSE SOCIETY
O'Connor Medical Building Auditorium
2101 Forest Avenue
San Jose
(408) 741-1372
Meets second Friday of each month at 7:30 P.M.

SOUTH BAY HERITAGE ROSE GROUP
1206 Curtiss Avenue
San Jose, CA 95125
(408) 298-7657
Meets four times a year; site varies. Call or write for information.

WATER GARDEN AND KOI CLUB OF THE SANTA CLARA VALLEY
St. Edward's Episcopal Church
15040 Union Ave
San Jose
(408) 287-3909
Meets second Friday of each month at 7:30 P.M.

NURSERIES AND PLANTS

BAY AREA IN GENERAL

CHAIN STORES

Warehouse/club megastores—Home Club, HomeBase, and the like—can have bargains for the alert shopper, but by the time you've acquired the necessary discernment you'll probably know some good reasons to shop at more locally based places. What's carried in warehouse chains tends toward standard assembly-line plants; the care they get once delivered to the retail outlets is iffy. Best strategy: find out what day they get deliveries and buy only newly delivered plants. Look sharp for yellowing leaves and for soil that's pulled away from the sides of the pot, betraying a plant that's been allowed to dry out completely once too often. Chances of getting good information are slim. I've seen faux pas like the strictly ornamental Mexican sage displayed in the culinary herbs rack.

When buying tools in a warehouse store, look beyond the price tag. The cheapest line of most things will be practically disposable, and prices on more substantial tools can be at best just a little lower than those at small businesses.

The PayLess drug and sundries chain has plant shops in most of its stores. Some of these are quite comprehensive, with stock from ground covers and edibles to trees and ornaments of varying virtue; some are strictly color and bagged potting soil vendors. The chain was bought out by the East Coast drugstore chain Rite-Aid in 1997, and some policies are changing. Frontline staff and salespeople have lost some benefits. This is not a good sign for those of us looking for skilled help in the nursery section. The corporation may have the sense to pay for skills, if nothing else, but the effect on the most interesting section of many stores remains to be seen.

ORCHARD SUPPLY HARDWARE
Locations throughout the Bay Area; see below.

Orchard Supply has expanded a lot in the last five years or so, and has suffered some of the usual problems expansion brings with it. Checkout can be slow; service and information can be uneven. You have a better chance of getting accurate info about plants if you flag down one of their nursery department specialists. What the stores stock, however, remains pretty good, especially if it's tools and soil amendments and such that you want. It's still the best place I know to get (surprise) an orchard ladder—a tripod ladder that's a good investment in safety if you're going to work on trees more than once a year. OSH is also good for other tree tools: pole saws (including the nefarious pole-mounted power saw), pruning hooks, fruit pickers, long-reach clippers, tree stakes and ties, and pruning-wound dressing, for which I'll grudgingly admit there may be a use somewhere in the world.

OSH's selection of gardening tools is better than most hardware stores', and better than some nurseries'. They also carry power tools, mowers and such, barbecues and grills, and some outdoor furniture. All this stuff is displayed handily for comparison-shopping; it's a good place to find out what's available. Their range of brands and prices is fairly broad.

OSH stores have attached nurseries. These are fair-to-middling: stock is almost entirely the standard landscape plants, with some individual variations that do seem geared toward the store's local climate. The Livermore store, for example, has a pretty good selection of heat-loving citruses. The plants are generally well cared for, and nursery staffers have information or will refer you to someone who does.

In the nursery department you can also get fencing, lumber, pavers, irrigation parts, cement mix by the bag, composts, mulches, gravel, and some really awful small statuary. They'll load it for you; just take the appropriate tag to the register, As Seen on TV. House-brand soil amendments are pretty good and reasonably priced.

All stores open Monday–Friday 8 A.M.–9 P.M.; Saturday 8 A.M.-8 P.M.; Sunday 8 A.M.–7 P.M. Generally wheelchair accessible.

1151 Andersen Drive, San Rafael
(415) 453-7288

2388 Buchanan Road, Antioch
(510) 778-6660

2050 Monument Boulevard, Concord
(510) 685-3000

1450 First Street, Livermore
(510) 455-8555

7884 Dublin Boulevard, Dublin
(510) 829-8470

1440 Fitzgerald Drive, Pinole
(510) 223-0542

1025 Ashby Avenue, Berkeley
(510) 540-6638

300 Floresta Boulevard, San Leandro
(510) 352-7124

117 Lewelling Boulevard,
San Lorenzo (510) 278-7300

5130 Mowry Avenue, Fremont
(510) 797-1723

5655 Jarvis Avenue, Newark
(510) 794-8300

2245 Gellert Boulevard,
South San Francisco (415) 878-3322

900 El Camino Real, Millbrae
(415) 873-5539

2110 Middlefield Road, Redwood City
(415) 365-7373

1010 Metro Center Boulevard,
Foster City (415) 525-2100

2555 Charleston Road,
Mountain View (650) 691-2000

7777 Sunnyvale-Saratoga Road,
Sunnyvale (408) 732-7734

3615 El Camino Real, Santa Clara
(408) 247-1915

1601 41st Avenue, Capitola
(408) 475-7701

751 East Capitol Expressway,
San Jose (408) 270-2600

20 West San Carlos Street, San Jose
(408) 297-7173

5365 Prospect Road, San Jose
(408) 446-0525

5651 Cottle Road, San Jose
(408) 578-0552

3000 Alum Rock Avenue, San Jose
(408) 259-5470

1130 Branham Lane, San Jose
(408) 267-6460

125 North Milpitas Boulevard,
Milpitas (408) 945-9555

And other locations, no doubt; they're multiplying rabbitly.

SLOAT GARDEN CENTER
Locations throughout the Bay Area; see below.

Sloat demonstrates that it is possible to be a chain operation and do things right, maybe it's because it's specifically a nursery chain, and the plants are its purpose, not an afterthought. Individual outposts vary only slightly in what they offer (with the exception of the Cove Center store in Tiburon, which is billed as "the organic Sloat's"), but there are variations enough to show that someone's paying attention. For example, the Third Avenue shop in San Francisco, just off Clement Street, has a rack of SLUG pamphlets in Chinese and a few so-labeled medicinal herbs. The whole chain is pretty strong on water gardens—plants, prefab ponds and kits, and equipment—and on containers, particularly pots that it imports from Malaysia, Vietnam, and Mexico. Many of these are quite handsome and distinctive and not what you'd expect; the Mexican high-fired pots, for example, have a grainy sandstone look, and are shaped more in the Italianate manner than in the usual Mexican terra-cotta style.

As for the quality of most of its plant assortments, Sloat hits the high end of mid-range. Stock invariably looks healthy on the whole, and includes the normal stuff and some surprises in every shop. Perennials include more than the usual warhorses, for example; edibles include Upstarts organics and heirloom tomatoes, and there's always some different herb there. Color includes Annie's Annuals.

Sloat issues a pretty good newsletter, which includes a schedule of the talks, lessons, clinics, book signings, and seminars that happen regularly at its various locations, on topics from garden design to less-toxic pest control to making moss baskets. There's a better-than-average selection of gardening books in most locations, too (bearing in mind that this usually means one display rack). Information tags, placards, and sheets are good and plentiful, and staffers, in my experience, either know their stuff or will point you to someone who does. There's an in-house landscape architect who runs Sloat's design service, which offers total garden master plans, or separate planting, irrigation, lighting, grading, and paving plans, as well as consultation and problem-solving on an hourly basis.

The "organic" Sloat, at the Cove Shopping Center in Tiburon, has some of the same stock as the other branches, with a concentration on organically raised edibles, less-toxic pest controls, organic soil amendments and fertilizers, herbs (including herb books and handsome bottles for herb vinegars and such), and critter-friendly gardens in general: butterfly feeders, ladybug bait, bat houses, and so on.

All locations have ornaments, fountains, trellises, stepping stones, and other decorative necessities, as well as soil amendments, fertilizers, mulch, and a reasonable assortment of good tools.

All open daily 9 A.M.–6:30 P.M. Extended spring and summer hours:
Sunday–Tuesday 8:30 A.M.–6:30 P.M.; Wednesday–Saturday 8:30 A.M.–8 P.M.
Wheelchair accessible.

---

327 Third Avenue (between Geary and Clement), San Francisco (415) 752-1614

2700 Sloat Boulevard, San Francisco (415) 566-4415

700 Sir Francis Drake Boulevard, Kentfield (415) 454-0262

279 Doherty Drive, Larkspur (415) 924-7390

657 East Blithedale Avenue, Mill Valley (415) 388-0102

401 Miller Avenue, Mill Valley
(415) 388-0365

1580 Lincoln Avenue, San Rafael
(415) 453-3977

2000 Novato Boulevard, Novato
(415) 897-2169

Cove Shopping Center, Tiburon
(415) 388-4721

SMITH & HAWKEN
Locations throughout the Bay Area; see below.

No homegrown business is the same after a corporate buyout, but changes at Smith & Hawken have been gradual and virtues have been retained. All the stores have a good selection of tools and equipment, potting soils, fertilizers, some botanical toiletries, and the sort of clothing only Martha Stewart would actually garden in. (I'll admit the Japanese farmer pants with built-in kneepads have always looked useful, and S&H does have good bargains on sale days.) Some stores have nurseries, and their plant material is first-rate. Some of those expensive tools are good investments, too; I have a so-called Poacher's Spade that I bought after they'd cleaned up the descriptive prose in the catalog, and it's just the thing for Berkeley clay soil. Historically there's been an unconditional lifetime warranty on tools and the like and they have delivered on it; I hope that will remain the case through any further corporate shuffling.

Garden accessories, gadgets, and ornaments range from baroque to rustic. Some of it's actually affordable, and some is irresistibly clever. Furniture is reliably elegant, and the teak stuff is plantation-grown, which is at least a step in the direction of virtue.

SMITH & HAWKEN
2040 Fillmore Street
San Francisco
(415) 776-3424
Monday–Friday 10 A.M.–7 P.M. Saturday 10 A.M.–6 P.M. Sunday 11 A.M.–6 P.M.
Wheelchair accessible

An urban sort of Smith & Hawken, with emphasis on containers and container plants.

SMITH & HAWKEN

1330 Tenth Street
Berkeley
(510) 527-1076
Monday–Saturday 10 A.M.–6 P.M. Sunday 11 A.M.–6 P.M.
Wheelchair accessible

Respectable nursery.

SMITH & HAWKEN OUTLET

1330 Tenth Street
Berkeley
(510) 525-2944
Friday and Saturday 10 A.M.–6 P.M.
Wheelchair accessible

This is a place for bargains in overruns, seasonal decor, and damaged items, some of which look right at home in a garden.

SMITH & HAWKEN

705 Stanford Shopping Center
Palo Alto
(650) 321-0403
Monday–Friday 10 A.M.–9 P.M. Saturday 10 A.M.–6 P.M. Sunday 11 A.M.–6 P.M.
Mostly wheelchair accessible, but some aisles are too narrow.

No nursery; containers, equipment, and accessories.

SMITH & HAWKEN

35 Corte Madera Avenue
Mill Valley
(415) 381-1800
Daily 9 A.M.–6 P.M.
Basically wheelchair accessible, vertical though the site is.

This one has an impressive nursery that segues into an engaging display garden.

SMITH & HAWKEN
26 North Santa Cruz Avenue
Los Gatos
(408) 354-6500
Monday–Friday 9 A.M.–7 P.M. Saturday 10 A.M.–7 P.M. Sunday 11 A.M.–6 P.M.
Wheelchair accessible; small nursery.

SAN FRANCISCO

ALEMANY FARMERS' MARKET
100 Alemany Boulevard
San Francisco
(415) 647-9423
FAX (415) 643-9514
Saturdays, dawn–dusk
Wheelchair accessible

Among the homey and the exotic produce on display you can also find veggie and herb starts, and the stuff being sold to eat is certainly inspiring. Best hunting will be in spring and summer. A good place to buy something you'd never heard of.

FLOORCRAFT GARDEN CENTER
550 Bayshore Boulevard
San Francisco
(415) 824-1900
Monday–Friday 9 A.M.–5:30 P.M. Saturday 9 A.M.–5 P.M. Sunday 10 A.M.–5 P.M.
Partly wheelchair accessible, but very crowded with plants and shelves. Shop is not accessible; it includes the tool, houseplant, and doodad sections.

Another nursery surrounded by a freeway, parking lots, and pavement generally, but managing to pay attention to the neighborhood microclimate. Among lots of veggie and herb seedlings here—including some organically grown—are varieties clearly chosen for foggy or windy conditions:

'Sweet 100,' 'Oregon Spring,' and 'Early Girl' tomatoes, lots of interesting greens, and so on. There are a lot of shade-loving plants, and some just plain gotta-have-it delights like *Clerodendron* vines. Water gardens, bamboos, trees, shrubs, and bedders; prices are moderate for all. There's a good assortment of tools and accessories, including the Solar Bell, an interesting version of the familiar farm Hotkap—just the thing to maximize sun on seedlings. Also lots of houseplants, including orchids, and containers. Crowded and jumping on a spring weekend, with staff dishing out information freely and fast.

GARDEN HOUND
1921 Clement Street
San Francisco
(415) 387-5608
FAX (415) 387-2868
Monday–Saturday 9 A.M.–5:30 P.M. (9 A.M.–6 P.M. in summer) Sunday 10 A.M.–5 P.M.
Mostly wheelchair accessible, though cramped.

One solution to fitting a garden—or a nursery—into a sliver of city ground is to go vertical, and Garden Hound's proprietor Thomas Ward seems to have done that almost accidentally. This breathing oasis in the Sunset district concrete looks as tall as it does wide, with lots of interesting vines, 'Lady Banks' roses, shrubs trained to standards, trellises, wall-hung planters, and plaques. Spread below are healthy annuals and perennials at good prices, a show of color and imagination. Houseplants in the shop are inexpensive too, including elegant varieties like sago palm, gardenia, and orchids. Tools, including bonsai tools and pots; plant foods and pesticides, including several of the Safer brand, and alternatives like snail-stopping copper tape; birdfeeders; and handsome accessories are all available; I particularly liked some handmade grapevine-and-antler baskets. Parking can be difficult on weekends, but this one's worth a few trips 'round the block.

The American Lung Association hands out lists and advice about plant allergens, which I will here pass on to you, with thanks to Dianna Rickey, Carlyn Halde, and the esteemed Elizabeth McClintock, who wrote the pamphlets I'm referring to. I'm glad to say that this is also one more reason not to waste ground on a lawn.

As any veteran wheezer or sneezer knows, the most bothersome pollens are wind-borne. You don't have to be a weatherman; if the wind's blowing from the east, you can count on a squeaky respiratory chorus to greet it in the Bay Area. Pollen can kite along for miles, but most stays pretty close to its plant of origin, say within a block. So under most circumstances, what's irritating your nose is right under it. If you're planting your own space, you have some control over what you breathe at home.

The culprit is usually something with small or inconspicuous flowers, often in catkins, often on species with separate male and female flowers or even separate male and female plants. It's the male flowers that get you; pollen, after all, is the plant equivalent of semen. Plants that are called "fruitless," like fruitless mulberry, or some plants that are cloned so as not to spread pesky invasive seeds, are selected for sex and are generally male; so are a few plants like gingko, whose fruits, borne on the female plant, are stinky or otherwise undesirable. (Gingko, though, is reputed to be nonallergenic.)

Big showy flowers are generally pollinated by insects, birds, or bats, as are flowers that are just plain odd like *Aristolochia* (which is pollinated by gnats that don't always make it out again) and those Rube Goldberg tropicals like the orchid that flashes a decoy female moth with which male moths try to mate. It's those innocent, sexless-looking, wind-pollinated grasses and junipers and such that cause the most grief.

Here's a partial list of the bad guys.

GRASSES: bentgrasses *(Agrostis* spp.*)*, Bermuda grass *(Cynodon dactylon)*, bluegrasses *(Poa* spp.*)*, bromes *(Bromus* spp.*)*, fescues *(Festuca* spp.*)*, oatgrasses *(Avena* spp.*)*, orchard grass *(Dactylis glomerata)*, rye grasses *(Lolium* spp.*)*, and several others. Of these, Bermuda grass is the worst, both because it's so common and invasive, and because it can flower and pollinate while still quite short, just days after mowing. The ALA recommends dichondra lawns, but those are awfully thirsty. It also recommends bunchgrasses (like our natives) or blends of perennial—not annual—rye grass, bluegrass, and tall fescue; the advantage is that these won't flower if you keep them mowed fairly short.

TREES AND SHRUBS: alders *(Alnus spp.)*, birch *(Betula spp.)*, bottle-brush *(Callistemon* spp.*)*, box elder *(Acer negundo)*, cottonwoods and poplars *(Populus spp.)*, true cypresses *(Cupressus spp.)*, elms *(Ulmus spp.)*, junipers *(Juniperus spp.)*, oaks *(Quercus spp.)*, olive *(Olea europaea)*, planetrees and sycamores *(Platanus spp.)*, privets *(Ligustrum spp.)*, sweetgum *(Liquidambar styraciflua)*, wattles *(Acacia* spp.*)*, walnuts *(Juglans* spp.*)*, and, to a lesser degree, ceanothus (I'd plant this anyway, since the flower's so glorious and its season so short). Pines put out a lot of pollen, but it's supposed to be insulated from contact with mucous membranes by its resin coat.

WEEDS: spiny cocklebur *(Xanthium spinosum)*, marijuana or hemp *(Cannabis sativa)*, pickleweed *(Salicornia* spp.*)*, English plantain *(Plantago lanceolata)*, ragweeds *(Ambrosia* spp., and who named them that?*)*, sagebrush *(Artemisia* spp.*)*, sheep sorrel *(Rumex acetosella)*, and Russian thistle *(Salsola* spp.*)*. Of particular interest in the ALA lists are "tumbleweed, pigweed, [green amaranth], lamb's-quarters, and other members of the Amaranthaceae and Chenopodiaceae families," since some, like spinach, are grown for food by gardeners. Even if you're allergic to their pollen, you shouldn't have problems if you just grow them for greens and harvest before they flower.

Plants that fewer of us are seriously allergic to include redwood *(Sequoia sempervirens)*, firs *(Abies* spp.*)*, silk oak *(Grevillea robusta)*, palms, maytens *(Maytenus* spp.*)*, podocarpus, Chinese tallow tree *(Sapium sebiferum)*, boxwoods *(Buxus* spp.*)*, and manzanitas *(Arctostaphylos* spp.*)*, to name a few. Anything that has a showy flower, like magnolia, silktree *(Albizia julibrissin)*, dogwood, hibiscus, or rhododendron (including azaleas), will probably be nonallergenic, but watch out for almonds, which for some reason are more irritating than other *Prunus* species.

The local American Lung Association is at 562 Mission Street, Suite 203, San Francisco, CA 94105, and I bet if you write them and send an SASE, they'll send you their leaflets "Hay Fever Plants of the San Francisco Bay Area" and "Sneezeless Landscaping." Until then, Gesundheit!

GOODMAN LUMBER COMPANY

445 Bayshore Boulevard
San Francisco
(415) 285-2800
Monday 8 A.M.–7:55 P.M. Tuesday–Sunday 8 A.M.–5:55 P.M.
Wheelchair accessible

The plant selection here is pretty much a token effort—the sort of thing you see everywhere because it's mass-produced. Sometimes a pedestrian plant is what you need; look for things on sale, as sale prices can be very good here. What you'll want to go here for is lumber for beds and other projects, building supplies, ready-made fencing and gates, tools, containers, outdoor furniture, and barbecue equipment.

THE GREENERY

3237 Pierce Street
San Francisco
(415) 567-4991
FAX (415) 292-7222
Daily 9 A.M.–6 P.M.
Wheelchair accessible, if you go out and come in again.

The Greenery's store walks that fine line between entertaining and overdone; the scent of potpourri is a bit thick, and one expects to see lace on the seed packets, but when you really need a pottery hippopotamus for the garden . . .

An inviting rear courtyard connects the shop with the nursery, which is almost next door (the assemblage holds a wine store in friendly embrace) and is a good place to clear your head and see a charming old fountain pool with goldfish, waterside plants, iron trellises and *tuteurs*, as well as ornaments elegant and funny. I particularly liked a cast-stone demon, reclining prone with chin in hand, taking the sun in the shrubbery. The plant material is healthy and well-chosen, not inexpensive, and abundant. A lot of it is clearly urban: tiny topiary herbs, climbers, small-space veggie starts. Plant foods, containers, some tools, and an assortment of decorative gravels and riverstones are sold by the scoop, too.

HORTICA

566 Castro Street
San Francisco
(415) 863-4697
FAX (415) 863-1024
Monday–Saturday 9 A.M.–7 P.M. Sunday 9 A.M.–6 P.M.
Not very wheelchair accessible; the outdoor plant space is on a quirkily
terraced slope.

Very urban, very urbane; I like this place a lot. There are ingenious ac-
commodations for every city-home situation, including having no outdoor space at all. Among its dizzying ranks of orchids and houseplants,
you can find indoor-loving bonsai and indoor pools and fountains, and
the tools and supplies they require—even koi! Outside on Hortica's slice
of ground are more bright ideas for small spaces: espaliered fruit trees, vines,
berries, regular outdoor bonsai, herbs, edibles, and ornamentals. The lot is
crammed with interesting material, and there's a sense of fun in most things,
including the multilevel water garden 'way in back. Containers, hangers,
seeds, tools, soil amendments, pond equipment, and good advice are available.

JEANNE'S BONSAI

43 Lake Street
San Francisco
(415) 387-9492
Monday–Saturday 10 A.M.–5 P.M.
Not wheelchair accessible; narrow basement passage, and
steps in yard.

Appointment advised, but look for the A-frame sign outside; if it's out, knock
on the door. A pair of San Francisco stores—Jeanne's Bonsai and Gifts, on
Lombard and on Polk—have retired to this tiny yard near Clement Street.
The approach is through a narrow basement hallway displaying bonsai tools,
books, and photographs. There are some very nice trees here, including some
at beginners' prices, like relatively tough junipers at about $25. There are
more refined Japanese black pines, too, and azaleas. If you don't want a finished tree, look at the babies for under $15; they're off to a good start.

KATSURA GARDEN

1825 Post Street (in Nihonmachi Mall)
San Francisco
(415) 931-6209
Monday–Saturday 10 A.M.–5:30 P.M. Sunday 11A.M.–5 P.M.
Not really wheelchair accessible.

This little bitty bonsai shop is also a stop for bonsai accoutrements like pots, soils, books, and tools, and for garden accessories, bamboos, and houseplants including orchids. Don't try to walk through here with your overloaded backpack or a toddler in a bumptious mood; I wouldn't try it in a powered chair, either.

LIVING GREEN PLANTSCAPE DESIGN

2 Henry Adams
(415) 864-2251
Monday–Friday 9 A.M.–5 P.M. Saturday 11 A.M.–5 P.M. Closed Sunday.
There are wheelchair barriers—one step, a very crowded space—but the staff is wheelchair-conscious and trained to assist and clear the way.

The jungle starts at the doorstep, but just wait till you get inside. This public-accessible (well, assuming the public doesn't require a lot of room) retail delight in a sea of to-the-trade-only decor stores near China Basin is an instant trip to five or six jungles at once, with outstandingly nifty artifacts from places like Borneo and Hawai'i and Kenya. There's a sort of instant Mayan ruin being engulfed by rampant vines; assorted gorgeous rocks and crystals; and plants so thick you can hardly move through them. The plants are mostly suited to indoor or courtyard use: bromeliads, tillandsias, orchids, ferns, palms, crotons, spathyphyllums, the odd succulent or two. There are water gardens, too, self-contained in some extraordinary handmade urns and basins, and fountains, some small enough for easy indoor use. One striking set of water-garden containers I've seen here was big enough to climb into. Each piece was round and made of crushed volcanic rock cast with fiberglass; they looked like raku dinosaur eggs, subtle and alien. The place is alive with big leaves and running water; a cage of Gouldian finches and well-chosen music complete the soundtrack. As well as retail sales,

Living Green offers design and maintenance, specializing in courtyard, terrace, and roof gardens.

At the other end of the building is Terrace Flowers, a retail florist that also sells containers and ornaments of the busted-cherub sort, architectural leftover bits, stone and mock-stone urns, and handsome rustic iron furniture. Terrace keeps about the same hours that Living Green does. It's worth a look while you're in the neighborhood.

THE PALM BROKER

1074 Guerrero Street
San Francisco
(415) 626-7256
http://www.palmbroker.com
Wednesday–Sunday 11 A.M.–6 P.M.
Wheelchair accessible, if you have rough-riding capability; it's a bumpy lot, not recently graded.

After being evicted from its last site to make way for an apartment building, the Palm Broker now inhabits a lot that's the site of a burned-down church. This is a Mission District oasis visible from blocks away. You'll find not only palms—small, large, skyscraping—but bamboos, bananas, and birds-of-paradise. Impressive cycads, tree ferns, and jacarandas rub elbows with queen palms and Senegal date palms, all in boxes and big planters scattered picturesquely about the lot. Plants of this size and rarity don't come cheap, but there are smaller bargains to be had from time to time. It's free to visit, and even a purchase is certainly cheaper than a plane ticket to the Canary Islands.

PLANT WAREHOUSE

1355 Bush Street
San Francisco
(415) 885-1515
Daily 10 A.M.–6 P.M.
Wheelchair accessible, though ramp may be obstructed by cars.

You can rent plants as well as buy them here; there's delivery ($15 within San Francisco) and maintenance service too. Mostly indoor plants at mostly reasonable prices; some spectacular large individuals for that rainforest look. There are also containers and some seeds, including herb seeds.

Plant Warehouse also has greenhouses in San Francisco (415-824-8828) and Half Moon Bay (415-726-0129).

PLANT'IT EARTH

2215 Market Street
San Francisco
(415) 626-5082
Tuesday–Saturday 10:30 A.M.–6:30 P.M. Sunday 11 A.M.–5 P.M. Closed Monday
Wheelchair accessible

Indoor hydroponics systems are good for growing legal plants too. You can, of course, grow your own drugs—coffee, for example—under lights. It's a good system for tropical plants, if you have the space and time; back in 1996, this little store was graced with a full-size banana tree that bore several hands of fruit, quite an impressive houseplant. Hydroenthusiasts claim that plants grow much faster in less space this way. I learned one other advantage from a heart-transplant beneficiary: hydroponics systems are even better than sterile potting soil arrangements for the immunologically compromised. It all seems a bit wonkish to this dirt gardener, but the results can be impressive.

In addition to the systems and parts—lights, pots, plumbing, growing media—this store sells fertilizers, organic soils, natural pest controls (less-toxic is a good idea indoors, of course), Seeds of Change seeds, and some plants. One interesting service is Club Orchid: Plant'It Earth will board your orchids all year, and call you to come fetch them when they're about to bloom. One wonders if this idea would apply to other species and phyla.

POTRERO GARDENS

17th and Texas Streets
San Francisco
(415) 861-8220
Monday–Saturday 9 A.M.–5 P.M. Sunday 10 A.M.–4 P.M.
Mostly wheelchair accessible.

A neighborhood of determined gardeners gets the nursery it deserves. In a cheerfully painted surround, you'll find multigrafted fruit trees, lots of roses, ornamentals and edibles, and a specialty: water gardens. There's a nice little demonstration pond full of horsetails and such, which has been known to attract the odd egret looking for a snack. Potrero Gardens also performs the public service of supplying free scenery for the Bottom of the Hill Club overlooking its lot. Shepherd's Garden Seeds, tools, soil amendments, containers, too. This is another place that pays attention to its microclimate—Potrero Hill has difficult soil in spots, but is one of SF's warmer neighborhoods—and sells plants that should do well there.

RED DESERT

1632-C Market Street
San Francisco
(415) 552-2800
Monday–Saturday 10 A.M.–6 P.M. Most Sundays 11 A.M.–5 P.M.
Technically wheelchair accessible, but the floor covering might complicate things.

A little wedge of a shop with a rather startling, if logical, interior decor. Your first step through the door is onto sand, which surrounds artful sandstone flags; display risers, rather elegantly calculated for the right angle of repose, are sand-covered so the effect is of cacti and succulents arranged on dunes. The stock is all plants, almost all cacti and other succulents, with the occasional dasylirion or sanseveria. There are striking, large euphorbias and ocotillo, the sort of thing you need a tough hide or a big space for. Smaller specimens are variously fuzzy, rocklike, or haloed in spines. A good place to shop for your favorite lover of odd things, or your favorite Martian.

NURSERY NEWSLETTERS

These can be at least worth the paper they're printed on. As with many of the preprinted information tags in nurseries, they're often sponsored by the wholesalers of handy chemicals and soil amendments, the 49'er and Ortho manufacturers. This is part of the reason you'll see advice to spray or drench or douse or dose with precautionary insecticides and fungicides, or add lots and lots of one particular soil mix to a new planting hole. The best newsletters go easy on this. Once you can sort out the commercials from the content, you might find good advice from nursery staffers who know the plants they deal with every day, notice that something new has hit the market, and offer seasonal reminders, bug and disease alerts, bright ideas, and recipes.

SUNSET GARDEN SUPPLY
320 Alemany Boulevard
San Francisco
(415) 648-4242
Daily 9 A.M.–5 P.M.
Not wheelchair accessible; mostly a vertical lot with
notchy little terraces.

"We were here before all these roads," a staffer told me. As hemmed in by concrete as Sunset Garden Supply is, with every square inch of the lot used for ingenious mazes and ranks of plants, the statement's believable. Sunset has been supplying its customers with bedding plants, water gardens, shrubs, and fruit trees, chosen for the exposures and lean soils of its neighborhood, since 1934. "Every year we pick out the biggest braggers to stock," he said— meaning that they seek out more seedlings of the same Gravenstein apples, for example, that proud clients bring to show off. Some things are stocked with a senior and stable clientele in mind: greengage plum trees, interesting fig varieties. Informational tagging is pretty good, but it's more fun to ask here, as there are plenty of stories to hear. Prices are modest, too. And it may be the smallest area in San Francisco in which it's possible to get lost.

UNDER THE SUN

655 Montgomery Street
San Francisco
(415) 982-0789
Monday 6 A.M.–6 P.M. Tuesday–Friday 7:30 A.M.–6 P.M.
Saturday and Sunday by appointment

Mostly cut flowers, but a small selection of orchids, bromeliads, ficus, and other houseplants. This is possibly the best place in the Financial District to get orchids at 6 A.M. Unless you encounter a furtive raincoat-clad early-morning orchid pusher, it's probably the *only* place in the Financial District to get orchids at 6 A.M.

YAHOO HERB'AN ECOLOGY

(415) 248-1840

Worms (red wigglers), worm-composting supplies, and custom-made worm boxes; books and good cheer. Temporarily without a storefront to call home, Yahoo is working at farmers' markets and street fairs, and by phone order. They'll deliver; there's a modest fee for delivery outside San Francisco.

EAST BAY

NAVLET'S NURSERY & GARDEN CENTERS

Locations throughout the East Bay; see below.

Garden supermarkets, complete with shopping carts and a promotional budget. The Concord location is particularly complete; all have a good assortment of basics and some surprises. This is the HQ of Buzz Bertolero, the Dirt Gardener, who (on the basis of an admittedly short sample) seems to cure everything by dumping some pesticide or other on it. No surprise, then, that you can find instruments of murder for almost any species imaginable, and when murder is necessary in the garden, nothing else will do. The places are varied enough, though, that Better Living through Chemistry isn't quite a theme; there's been more emphasis on less-toxic alternatives over the last few years, and they do sell CCOF-certified organic veggie seedlings, and a praiseworthy variety of heirloom tomatoes.

The Concord store has a particularly broad variety of citrus trees, including several species on 'Flying Dragon' dwarfing rootstock. All sell bareroot fruit trees in season, some very inexpensive one-gallon shrubs and perennials, bedders, shade trees, and edibles. Hardware includes tools, prefab fencing, gates, and trellises; edging (including that nasty plastic benderboard stuff) and brick trim; stepping stones, pavers, and retaining-wall components. Ornaments of various sorts, pools, fountains, birdbaths, and feeders, too.

All open daily 8 A.M.–5:30 P.M.
http://www.dirtgardencr.com
Generally wheelchair accessible.

6740 Alhambra Avenue, Martinez (510) 935-9125

1250 Monument Boulevard, Concord (510) 685-0700

1333 Newell Avenue, Walnut Creek (510) 935-7373

800 Camino Ramon, Danville (510) 837-9144

46100 Warm Springs Road, Fremont (510) 657-7511

ENCINAL NURSERY
2057 Encinal Avenue
Alameda
(510) 522-8616
Friday–Wednesday 9 A.M.–5:30 P.M., Closed Thursday

Once past the demonstration garden with its watercourse, look for a quite diverse selection of indoor plants (including coconut palms and one-gallon cycads), small trees, and potentially big trees like limber pine and dawn redwood. There are also already big trees: junipers and jacarandas in fifteen-gallon pots, for example. Perennials include a good choice in four-inch size;

annuals include lots of color and a reasonable assortment of edibles. You'll see tools, ornaments, indoor fountains, and some pretty good containers, along with the usual necessities like fertilizers and pesticides.

THOMSEN'S GARDEN CENTER
1113 Lincoln Avenue
Alameda
(510) 522-3265
Daily 9 A.M.–5 P.M. Closed Thursday

This is a nursery with a personal touch, both in the plants it stocks—Annie's Annuals, Jackson and Perkins roses, small trees, and shrubs like mountain laurel, along with climbers and ground covers and a lively herbaceous assortment—and in the sort of service a client can expect. I've watched the sort of transaction in which a customer says. "Help me fill this pot," and overheard informed chat about plant diseases and what to do about them. Of particular interest are small-space plants and accessories, four-inch perennials, and indoor plants. You'll also find fountains, containers, and ornaments, and sundries like fertilizers and a good assortment of less-toxic pest controls.

FLOWERLAND NURSERY
1330 Solano Avenue
Albany
(510) 526-3550
Daily 9 A.M.–5 P.M. Closed some holidays
Wheelchair accessible

A modest neighborhood nursery with charm and a few surprises. Staff and owner are friendly and know their plants. You can get perennials, sod, bedders, edibles, trees and shrubs, hand tools, containers, soil amendments, pesticides—all the basics—and firewood in season, too. A flea market table, which holds those half-price skinny puppies that softhearted gardeners love to take home and make happy again, makes Flowerland easier on the budget.

BERKELEY HORTICULTURAL NURSERY

1310 McGee Avenue
Berkeley
(510) 526-4704
Daily 9 A.M.–5:30 P.M.
Wheelchair accessible, mostly

An East Bay flagship family nursery, whose contributions to the community have included the introduction of fuchsias and Victor Yool, aka Dr. Hort. You can find just about anything here: trees, shrubs, vines, perennials, grasses, ground cover, shade plants, edibles, color, and an excellent range of California natives. What you won't find much of is the ordinary. Trees can include rarities like *Franklinia altamaha*, the "lovely phantom" of North American trees; there's always something you've never tasted among the veggie starts; and among the perennials you'll find the one you wanted, in a variety that you hadn't thought of. The four-inch perennials display is a good place to see what's new in the trade. There's an interesting choice of houseplants, too, including orchids and succulents; a seasonally changing array of bulbs; Annie's Annuals; ornaments, trellises, tools, soil amendments, and so on. Here's where to shop if you've decided to grow your own cup of tea or chew of khat. Information tags and cards are plentiful and thorough, and of course there's expertise at hand from a historically smart staff. The demo garden alone is worth finding a parking space to see, and sometimes the place is further graced by appetizing aromas from the block of food shops and restaurants around the corner.

THE DRY GARDEN

6556 Shattuck Avenue
Berkeley
(510) 547-3564
Tuesday–Saturday 10 A.M.–5 P.M. Sunday 11 A.M.–4 P.M.
Wheelchair accessible, some tight spaces

A quirky and original outfit, the Dry Garden started as a succulents specialty shop, branched out into the drought-tolerants that suddenly get fashionable during a drought, and never looked back. You can find seriously odd plants here, succulents and Baja and Alta California natives, trees, vines, shrubs, and unclassifiables like Giant Island Coreopsis, a plant as Thurberian as its name. You just can't get through this place in a hurry if you're paying attention; there are Marcia Donahue's and Mark Bulwinkle's fanciful and hilarious sculptures, found objects, the right containers for succulents, always something unexpected. When the wind's right, you can bask in the inspirational aura of Flint's Barbecue, across the street, while you browse. This place has the best company T-shirt in California—I'm no fan of advertising but I own two of them. Go ahead, ask what a hortisexual is. Buy the shirt if you think you are one.

EAST BAY NURSERY

2332 San Pablo Avenue
Berkeley
(510) 845-6490
Tuesday–Saturday 8:30 A.M.–5 P.M. Closed Sunday, Monday
Wheelchair accessible

The gardener's supermarket in Berkeley. Prices are moderate, stock is varied, and there's lots of it. A stroll through the rows of big trees is inspiring. Tags and information labeling are good, and the staff is generally helpful and informed. Lots of water-garden plants, succulents, perennials and rock-garden plants, bedders and specimens. There's usually something new and interesting up near the entrance in a display garden. Shepherd's Garden Seeds, tools, soil amendments and fertilizers, containers, houseplants, and ornaments, too. This is another family-owned small business, though it's big as nurseries go. Depending on your attitude toward Christmas and certain sorts of aesthetic extravagance, the annual display of ornaments is either arresting or arrestable.

MAGIC GARDENS

729 Heinz Street
Berkeley
(510) 644-1992
Monday–Saturday 9 A.M.–5:30 P.M. Sunday 10 A.M.–5 P.M.
Wheelchair accessible

After a few lean years, this innovative nursery in industrial-gentrified south-west Berkeley is living up to its early promise. Magic Gardens boasts of having the largest perennial selection in the region and it just could be true. It's a good place for new or old and interesting plants like Annie's Annuals—not cheap in their four-inch pots, but species and varieties you won't find just anywhere. Magic Gardens' own setup is a good demonstration that gardening is possible anywhere: heaps of soil mix, piled right on the tarmac of the former parking lot and held handsomely in place by rocks, are planted and interplanted with cheerful variety. The informational tag system sometimes breaks down, but what's there is useful, and staff are knowledgeable and friendly. There's an assortment of earth-friendly garden aids like copper anti-snail tape and (more dubious) rock powder, and varied and interesting classes listed in a monthly newsletter.

NATIVE HERE NURSERY
101 Golf Course Drive
Tilden Park
Berkeley
(510) 549-0211
Fridays 9 A.M.–12 P.M. Second Saturday of each month 10 A.M.–1 P.M.
Other Saturdays as volunteers are available.
Partly wheelchair accessible; this is an almost ungraded, slopey, rough bit of ground on a hillside.

This nursery, a project of the local chapter of the California Native Plant Society, has a mission. It specializes not just in native plants, but in local genotypes. Charli Danielsen propagates plants from various Bay Area locations for native-plant lovers, home gardeners, and restoration gardeners; every plant is labeled with its species name and the location its parent or parents came from. There are no cultivars here; all plants are offspring (usually from seed) of plants native to Alameda and Contra Costa Counties, and they're kept separate according to where they come from. Native Here will custom-grow plants from the area nearest your garden; this is one way to ensure perpetuation of even those local species and subspecies and varieties and variations whose distinctive qualities haven't been catalogued yet. Restoration can take place on a small scale—a yard or two—too. Acknowledging our own ignorance and giving it (and the rest of the world) elbow room is an indispensable step toward learning more. Besides, some of these honeys are just too good to lose.

Watch for a native vegetation-management calendar to be published by Ms. Danielsen in collaboration with other native-plant experts.

WESTBRAE NURSERY
1272 Gilman Street
Berkeley
(510) 526-7606
Monday–Saturday 8:30 A.M.–5 P.M. Sunday 9 A.M.–4:30 P.M.
Wheelchair accessible

Another family-owned small enterprise, with the advantages these typically have—they deal with local growers and innovators and can work with small suppliers with a minimum of bureaucratic fuss, so the good stuff gets here first, like organically grown seeds and vegetable and herb starts, often of interesting varieties and often ahead of the mass market. Their locally grown seedling varieties are best suited to local growing conditions, too. There's a good assortment of houseplants, orchids, and tchotchkes; a small selection of containers (in which you're likely to find a good one); and outdoors, the offerings tend to be practical—lots of food and easy landscaping. Both are probably inevitable; the place is surrounded by two bakeries, a deli, and a garden-art gallery, The Garden Gallery/A New Leaf Landscaping. Friendly and knowledgeable staff.

YABUSAKI'S DWIGHT WAY NURSERY
1001 Dwight Way
Berkeley
(510) 845-6261
Monday–Saturday 8 A.M.–5 or 5:30 P.M. Sunday 9 A.M.–4 P.M. Closed Thursday
Partly wheelchair accessible; very tight spaces, and office/shop has steps.

A personal favorite. This second-generation family nursery features lots of bonsai starts—two-inch and four-inch babies from Lone Pine Nursery, and gallon-size trees shaped a little and ready for serious work—and completely trained bonsai. The prices are reasonable, especially considering some really good styling. A good selection of bonsai pots, too, and tools, equipment, accessories, and Dwight Way's custom bonsai soil mix, as well as ingredients to make your own. They offer repotting, pruning, and other services for bonsai—everything except boarding.

Dwight Way also carries the nursery standards—veggie starts, bedding plants, annuals, perennials, shrubs, trees—and the buyer here has an eye for handsome and unusual plants. Expect surprises; among the herb seedlings in spring you'll find shiso, or Japanese lemon pepper, a fine-leafed woody shrub.

Other finds are bamboos, fruit and flowering fruit trees, nicely shaped landscape pines, and a good lot of indoor plants, including indoor bonsai. The informational tags are good, and anything not on those is easy to find out from friendly and knowledgeable staff.

R & M POOL PATIO AND GARDENS
6780 Marsh Creek Road
Clayton
(510) 672-0207
Monday–Saturday 9 A.M.–6 P.M. Sunday 10 A.M.–5 P.M.
Wheelchair accessible

This charming business started out as strictly swimming pools and pool supplies, and branched into gardening, particularly poolside gardening, with its recent acquisition of an abandoned nursery. Impressive amounts of dirt were moved by hand to construct a centerpiece waterfall, pools, planted berms, and paths in a meandering demonstration garden. Plant choices vary from droughty sun-lovers to container plants for a shady oasis. Prices are reasonable. You can still get pool supplies and pools—both the swimming and the ornamental variety—and the sort of furniture one associates with them. A sculptor in the family has contributed some inspiring woven-twig arches and trellises, as well as the stone fascia of the waterfall. There's a gift shop, too.

CHOOSING A TREE

Picking out the right tree in a nursery can be confusing, and a tree is (one hopes) a long-lived investment. A real nursery that values its clients and its reputation will be careful to steer you right, but an informed consumer will generally fare best anywhere. Choose a tree with a bigger caliper—trunk thickness—over a taller one, even if it costs a bit more. Look for healthy color, which can depend on species but is generally a deep, not-hysterical green. A yellowing conifer in particular is a bad gamble, as conifers tend to be moribund before they show poor health. Nodes—the places where buds and twigs and branches emerge—should be relatively close together. Some pruning for shape is a good thing, but there should be no stubs or bark scars from this. Unless you're looking for special effects, a tree should be fairly symmetrical, and should never have been topped (beheaded). All its twigs should be plump, resilient, and unwrinkled. Touch it; its leaves should be a little cooler than the air around it. (This is subtle, and it helps to touch a lot of trees to educate your senses.) There should be no gap between the soil and the sides of the container the plant is in; a gap both allows water to run off without wetting the roots and suggests that the plant was allowed to dry out a lot at some point. The best idea, as with so many such things, is to find a healthy individual of the species you want, in the wild or in someone's garden, and have it in mind for comparison.

SUNSET COLOR
1435 San Ramon Valley Boulevard
Danville
(510) 831-3574
Tuesday–Sunday 8:30 A.M.–4:30 P.M.
Wheelchair accessible

Color indeed: Sunset specializes in geraniums, pelargoniums, and other perennials, all of which have great color in common. They're propagated here, which means a low price for most, and a good chance of finding something you've never seen before because it's not on the general market yet. The stock includes lots of scented-geranium varieties, drought-tolerant plants, and the sort of quirky find you run across in a propagating nursery that has a plant fancier at the helm; I found a yerba mansa, for example: a California marsh native whose startling white coneflower blooms have arrested my attention in the wild, though I haven't seen it in retail sale often. Prices are great; tagging is pretty good, and staffers are friendly and helpful.

ADACHI NURSERY

5166 Sobrante Avenue
(at Valley View and Sobrante Avenues, off Appian Way)
El Sobrante
(510) 223-6711
Daily 9 A.M.–5:30 P.M.
Wheelchair accessible, though some aisles are narrow.

Still a family business, this is the single branch remaining after the somewhat larger El Cerrito store gave way to a Home Depot. The moderately priced veggie starts include some interesting salad and stir-fry greens, and other seedlings include handy things like very low priced, small pelargoniums and fuchsias, good for overplanting windowboxes. This is a good place to look for Asian "apple" pears, with good informative tags to help match pollinators and such. Bonsai starts, some of them nicely shaped already, mingle with finished bonsai, some very well done for commercial stock. Good assortment of bonsai pots and tools, too, along with ingenious Japanese-style garden tools.

GROVE WAY BONSAI NURSERY

1239 Grove Way
Fremont
(510) 537-1157
Thursday–Saturday 8:30 A.M.–5:30 P.M.
Not really wheelchair accessible; the front part of the garden is tightly packed, and the back, where the trees are, is reached through the shop, which has steps. There's a locked gate that might be usable on request.

John Uchida just might have the best retail-sale bonsai in the Bay Area. I have never seen anything to match some of his California native junipers, outside of bonsai shows and the collections of some very good local artists and bonsai fanciers. His other species don't disappoint by comparison, either. He has Japanese black pine, shimpaku juniper, maples, wisteria, and lots of others, in sizes and ages from thready seedling to mighty matriarch. You'll also find choice containers, bonsai soil mix and amendments, tools and wire; stone lanterns and similar ornaments; *suiseki*; and current and back issues of *Bonsai Today* magazine. There are plants other than bonsai, too, notably bamboos. Mr. Uchida also runs a landscaping business, installs sod, and will prune your bonsai for you.

MISSION ADOBE GARDEN CENTER

36501 Niles Road
Fremont
(510) 796-7575
Daily except Tuesday 9:30 A.M.–4:30 P.M.
Wheelchair accessible, but walks are graveled; the going might be tough in some areas.

Big shade and flowering trees, palms, and variations on standard species, like 'San Gabriel' nandina and several shades of flowering cherry. Five-gallon fruit trees are reasonably priced, and a good size to start with; for one thing, you don't need to dig so big a hole as for larger saplings, and they catch up with their older brethren in a few years anyway. There's a reasonable assortment of good perennials and color here, and succulents, some edibles, bonsai, sod, and houseplants (including orchids), and there are tools and supplements to take care of it all.

HARRY'S NURSERY

3925 Mount Diablo Boulevard
Lafayette
(510) 283-3830
Friday, Saturday, Monday–Wednesday 9:30 A.M.–4 P.M. Sunday 10 A.M.–4 P.M.
Closed Thursdays
Mostly not wheelchair accessible; it's on a terraced slope.

Its immediate neighbors are body shops and cell-phone brokers, but what overshadows Harry's most impressively is the peach-colored combined mass of condos and the Lafayette Park hotel. The nursery is unassuming in contrast. Its lot is long and narrow enough for a spaghetti farm, and every inch has been exploited with an uphill maze of plants. A clear specialty here is small maples—Japanese maples, Amur maples, and more. Prices (where you can find them—tags are pretty sparse) aren't super-low, but the trees are healthy, handsomely shaped, and worth it. Don't quit at the gift and pot shop—bonsai pots and ikebana vases, mostly—but walk around to the right and climb the hill for a look at pots of roses and . . . cabbages? Cabbages. Also fruit trees, including rarities in the trade like greengage plum. The perennial assortment includes lots of irises, terrestrial orchids, and echinacea.

ORCHARD NURSERY AND FLORIST

4010 Mount Diablo Boulevard
Lafayette
(510) 284-4474
Daily 9 A.M.–5:30 P.M.
Wheelchair accessible

Great big dressy nursery that has practically everything: stone obelisks, greyhound-sized gryphons, containers, containers for containers (racks and hooks), books, tools, fountains, ponds, trellises, outdoor furniture, piped-in (and -out) music, and bottled coyote urine. (Apparently it's a deer repellent; I don't want to think about how they collect it.)

Oh yes, plants. Orchard has those, too—lots of them. Topiary trees, normal trees, bedders, specimens, veggie starts, shrubs, water and pondside plants, ground covers, bonsai starts, succulents, vines . . . and so on. Informational tags are very good and are supplemented by accurate and to-the-point Gro-Sheets—free one- or two-page leaflets on subjects like deer-resistant plants (in case your coyote runs dry), what to plant under native live oaks, composting, and fire-resistant planting. The staffers seem to know their stuff, too, and are solicitous without being intrusive. Don't miss the little house on the parking lot, a refined shop full of ornaments for indoors and out; there are good things there even if you don't much like cuteness.

ALDEN LANE NURSERY

981 Alden Lane
Livermore
(510) 447-0280
Monday–Friday 9 A.M.–6 P.M. Saturday and Sunday 8:30 A.M.–5:30 P.M.
Wheelchair accessible

This is the very model of a modern major nursery, with information general, specific, never cursory. Also a great variety of bareroot fruit trees, berries, wine grapes and table grapes, and stuff like four- or five-in-one grafted apple or plum trees, some already cordoned. Roses aplenty. Take a close look at Alden's intriguing demo gardens, including a daybreak garden, hummingbird-butterfly garden, shade garden, and "Alden Pond." The grounds are graced by a grove of gorgeous mature deciduous oaks, which have been integrated into the design and function of the nursery. Good explanatory signs and tags abound, as do to-the-point educational flyers on topics like planting technique, intensive small-space orchards, IPM, and even a referral list for services and hard-to-find plants at other nurseries. Educational work includes a Kids' Club that gives garden classes all summer to kids from five to twelve years old, for $2.50 per class. Proprietor Jacquie Williams-Courtwright hosts the daily *Valley Gardener* show on cable TV, channel 30 in the Livermore cable area. Spring and fall events include art, music, antique-farm-implement demos, and walnut hulling and drying demos in the working orchard next to the nursery grounds. Signing the mailing list gets you a fairly useful monthly newsletter, with tangible rewards like coupons for free seedlings (a can of food for a local relief agency is requested with the coupon) and a monthly raffle.

THE ORCHID RANCH

1330 Isabel Avenue
Livermore
(510) 447-7171
Hours vary; all are open Friday and Saturday.

Three orchid growers under three roofs in one place. The results of this alliance are dazzling, especially in late winter through spring, when the various orchids bloom en masse. Orchids Orinda specializes in phalenopsis orchids (and you might get a dose of opera and an extemporaneous economics lecture with your flowers); Tonkin Orchids, in paphiopedalums; Fordyce Orchids, dendrobiums, paphs, and a number of outdoor-living orchid species. All have reasonable prices and healthy and interesting stock, as they do their own breeding and hybridizing. An unlikely oasis in a dry, open space that's rapidly being engulfed by the developmental tide.

COTTAGE GARDEN PLANTS
2680 Franklin Canyon Road
Martinez
(510) 946-9136
cottage@value.net
Daily 9 A.M.–4 P.M.
Wheelchair accessible, but rough and in spots deeply mulched or boggy.

This one's fun, including the drive down Franklin Canyon Road to get here. It's one of those havens for wild birds, with assorted species of swallow and hawk and woodpecker and passerines, and butterflies, too—which is no accident; one of Tim Torres' specialties is butterfly habitat, and he works with civic bodies to establish more of that in other places. Other specialties, to judge just from masses of stock, are daylilies, bunchgrasses, true geraniums, and such esoteric California natives as desert willow. There are boxed and potted trees, many of them conifers; multigrafted fruit trees, whose quantity depends on the season; Japanese maples and dogwoods and vines, lots of clematis among them; herbs, perennials of all sorts, some bedders. Strictly plants here, and worth the trip. Mr. Torres is enthusiastic and expert about his work, and works with the likes of Ruth Bancroft herself in propagating rarities.

MORAGA GARDEN CENTER
1400 Moraga Road
Moraga
(510) 376-1810
Wednesday–Monday 9 A.M.–5 P.M. Closed Tuesdays.

Closed for 2 weeks in January.
Mostly wheelchair accessible, though tight in spots.

"We sell knowledge," says owner Ken Murakami. This twenty-five-year-old family business sells plants raised here or chosen with a knowing eye, and at excellent prices—look for particular bargains in trees and in four-inch perennials like lavender and Cleveland sage. There are interesting veggie starts, particularly salad greens; shrubs and bedders; tools and supplements; and handy things for the area like gopher-proof root baskets. Murakami works with the UC Berkeley Botanical Garden and UC Davis in testing and evaluating plant varieties for local conditions. He's the sort of nurseryman whose clients bring him flowers and questions and get accurate answers in return.

EMPTIES

A big garden project or a lot of little ones can result in a stack of black plastic gallon-size or larger containers, more than you'll ever need. They are handy for the sort of plant you want to rotate into and out of a prominent position in a cachepot or an urn at the door, say, or in- and outdoors. When that stack starts to topple, you might look around for a nursery that will take them back. Some return them to their wholesalers for a deposit, like bottles. Some nurseries, though, can't rely on their wholesalers to ransom their cans; some just don't have the space to spare. Ask.

Nurseries that solicit gallon cans include Yerba Buena, off Skyline Drive in Woodside; they do their own propagation and handle a *lot* of plants. Other than commercial propagating nurseries, there are groups like the California Native Plant Society, Tilden Park Botanic Garden, and several of the local community college horticulture departments that gladly accept nursery cans as donations (CNPS likes intact, square, four-inch pots, too). Don't expect a deposit return unless you were charged one, of course; one exception is A to Z Tree Nursery in San Jose, which pays small deposits for five-gallon and larger cans.

ACE GARDEN CENTER

4001 Grand Avenue
Oakland
(510) 652-9143
Monday–Friday 8:30 A.M.–6 P.M. Saturday 9 A.M.–6 P.M. Sunday 10 A.M.–4 P.M.

This one's clearly stocked with the small urban garden in mind. It has lots of vines; small shrubs, many trained to space-saving standards; and a few trees, including dwarf citrus and flowering varieties. There are basic edibles and herbs, Annie's Annuals, Jackson and Perkins roses, and some adventurous perennials and pond plants. Thorough plant and information labeling demonstrates some resident expertise. Nonliving stock includes small fountains, hooks and freestanding hangers, some handsome small terra-cotta decor, very civilized pots and baskets, Birkenstock garden clogs, Felco pruners and replacement parts for them, bonsai tools, soil amendments and fertilizers, and a gadget called the Pottery Trainer that drains containers standing on decks so they don't rot the wood under them.

BROADWAY TERRACE NURSERY

4340 Clarewood Drive
Oakland
(510) 658-3729
Monday–Saturday 9 A.M.–5:30 P.M. Sunday 9 A.M.–5 P.M.
Wheelchair accessible

A small nursery on a pie-slice lot surrounded by a high-end restaurant, a food market, a gas station, and stump souvenirs of the Oakland Hills fire. Like most such businesses, it competes with the big chains not on a price basis, but with service, variety, and information; owner Helen Servidor answers questions with expertise and candor, and more information than usual is available on the plant tags posted with every species and many varieties. In spring, look for balled-and-burlapped dogwoods, roses, rhodies, and multigraft fruit trees, all chosen with the local microclimate in mind. Much of the information comes courtesy of a loyal customer base, always a great feedback mechanism for a nursery.

COST PLUS NURSERY/HOUSEPLANT MARKET

101 Clay Street
Oakland
(510) 465-6384
FAX (510) 465-6126
Monday–Friday 9 A.M.–9 P.M. Saturday 9 A.M.–8 P.M. Sunday 10 A.M.–7 P.M.
Wheelchair accessible with some maneuvering; go to the end of the
store's sidewalk.

Possibly keeping the latest hours of any local nursery (unless you count the
PayLess/Thrifty/Rite-Aid/Whoever Bought Them Out This Year at 51st
and Broadway), this mostly houseplant market also sells a few outdoor stalwarts and herbs. The indoor choices include orchids of several species, cacti
and succulents, palms, and some stately and sizable individuals. You can get
plant food, a few pesticides, containers, clever ornaments, and hangers, and
they deliver locally for free. Special orders taken, too.

GOMES NURSERY

9875 MacArthur Boulevard (between 98th and 99th)
Oakland
(510) 632-7142
Tuesday–Saturday 8:30 A.M.–5 P.M. Sunday 10 A.M.–4 P.M. Closed Mondays
Wheelchair accessible

Family-run and fifty-four years old, Gomes Nursery is up against the ob-
stacles common to such places: changing surroundings, an emigrating customer base, and competition from big wholesale chains. This is one to get to
quickly, before the retail arm of the business folds entirely. Azaleas you won't
see anywhere else, gorgeous specimens mature and flourishing enough to be
trees, striking for their structure as much as for their flowers. Some of the big
ones in the greenhouse are not for sale; they earn their keep as rentals for
events like Macy's spring flower display. There are other delights: lots of
cymbidium orchids, lewisias, and a good selection of Japanese maples, including bonsai starts and mature bonsai, rather handsomely worked. The
landscape trees in general—the maples especially—have been initially
shaped; for a tree of good caliper that's off to a good start, I'd look here first.

THORNHILL NURSERY
6250 Thornhill Drive
Oakland
(510) 339-1311
Daily 9 A.M.–5:30 P.M.
Mostly wheelchair accessible, though part of the display area is on a slope
with narrow paths and a step or two. Some tight spaces.

This one is worth a visit just to look around, and you'll know it as soon as
you walk through the splendid front gate and notice the jolly cement 'gator
in the stream that runs past it. It's a dressy place: Martha Stewart with a
sense of humor. There's a lot here for the small urban or Japanese-influenced
garden, including sixty varieties of Japanese maple and similar species like
Acer Japonicum (Japanese maple is *A. palmatum*), some in four-inch pots. There
are very formal-looking topiaries, succulents, annuals and perennials, well-
shaped small landscape trees, hayrack planters, ornaments from arty to
amusing, a discriminating choice of hand tools, and the usual garden supplements and soil conditioners. Some of the trees on the property are stunningly
well-pruned and worth studying.

YUMAE NURSERY
1433 55th Avenue
Oakland
(510) 534-1834
Tuesday–Saturday 8 A.M.–5 P.M.
Wheelchair accessible

In the family and in the neighborhood since 1929, Yumae boasts twenty
varieties of chili peppers, and grows its own stock, including big tomatoes,
variously hued bell peppers, and eggplants, suited to east Oakland's warm
microclimate. There are lots of standard yard-covers like vinca, plus a few
interesting citrus trees. The landscape trees have been given good initial shape
via pruning; a few are ready for instant-effect use. Outside the veggie seedling section, informational tags are minimal, but good advice is freely given.

MCDONNELL NURSERY
196 Moraga Way
Orinda
(510) 254-3713
Daily 8:30 A.M.–5 P.M.
Wheelchair accessible

What distinguishes this small nursery from the big discount guys is service, says its proprietor. He'll deliver almost anywhere—even west of the hills—and help with decisions, with good advice on what to plant under the area's plentiful and prized live oaks, for example. This is actually a big deal; the wrong underplantings can have fatal results, as California live oaks are quite intolerant of summer irrigation, and their roots reach farther than most people imagine. He also strongly prefers to deal with small local wholesale growers, for variety and quality of stock. Good idea. McDonnell sells shade and fruit trees, including a good selection of citrus, shrubs, specimens, and bedders, as well as tools, containers, some interesting ornaments, soil, and supplements.

HIGHLAND GARDEN CENTER AND ROCK CITY
1625 Buchanan Road
Pittsburg
(510) 432-2282
Monday–Friday 8:30 A.M.–5:30 P.M. Saturday 8 A.M.–6 P.M. Sunday 8:30 A.M.–5 P.M.
Mostly wheelchair accessible, if rough; the plant display area slopes off pretty sharply toward a streambed in the rear.

See Rock City for rocks, soil amendments, gravels, and mulches; also for statuary (some fairly alarming, though I have to admit liking a concrete gold panner trailing a stream from his pan, a design more clever than the standard puking cherub), fountains, and trees (including fruit trees that thrive on the warm side of the hills), and some calculated risks like tropical guava. There are shade trees, too; sod and ground covers; and seeds for dichondra, clover, onions, beans, and other vegetables. Most of the plants here are gallon-size or larger. The staff is competent and friendly to amateurs, and can heave enormous rocks around in a most impressive, if unassuming, manner.

KEN'S NURSERY

2364 Road 20 (at San Pablo)
San Pablo
(510) 234-7541
Monday–Friday 8 A.M.–5:30 P.M. Saturday and Sunday 9 A.M.–4 P.M. Closed
Wednesday
Front area is wheelchair accessible, but . . .

The best stuff is out back, on the deck that overlooks the creek: sizable pines, live oaks, pittosporums, and camellias trained in the Japanese style, some for around ten years. If you need an instant focal point and good example, here's where to get it. The nursery has been on this site since 1952, and run by the same couple, who also do the training. There are lots of roses in spring, shrubs and trees, and bedding plants; you'll also find containers, ornaments, and supplements. Informational tagging is minimal, but the owners are pleased to talk about their stock. Worth a stop just to see some of the specimen trees and watch the creek for a few minutes.

LEMURIA NURSERY

13065 San Pablo Avenue
San Pablo
(510) 234-3781
Daily 9 A.M.–5 P.M.
Wheelchair accessible

Why "Lemuria"? I'd hoped to find plants from the Lost Continent, but Erik and Peter Fink's grandfather apparently named his nursery after the Lemurian Society, one of those high-minded discussion clubs, to which he belonged. He *was* an archaeologist, though. The current owners make the most of their low-rent, small-nursery situation by dealing with adventurous local growers, soliciting feedback from customers, and indulging a fancy for Japanese maples, stocking "oh, fifty, sixty varieties" that they buy on annual shopping trips to growers in Northern California and Oregon. They propagate a small number of plants for sale themselves, too, in a small area in back of the nursery; check this spot out for things you've never heard of. Prices are moderate to low for perennials, annuals, veggie starts (including seed potatoes and onion sets) and ornamentals. One informal specialty is perennials in small sizes, like four-inch pots, which are cheaper to buy, easier to plant, and catch up with their larger kin quickly. This makes it easier to do your own experimentation.

HIRAMINE NURSERY
32727 Alvarado-Niles Road
Union City
Daily 8:30 A.M.–5 P.M.
(510) 471-0272
Wheelchair accessible, but walks are graveled.

A good place to look for a feature tree that's already been given a start toward a striking shape. There are landscape trees shaped in the Japanese manner: black pine, juniper, maples, Atlas cedar, podocarpus, even olive, and shrubs like box-wood. It's a good place to look at examples if you already have a tree you want to reshape, too. You can also find Japanese garden trappings, honest bonsai and bonsai equipment, and a range of other plants from veggies, fruit trees, and grapes to dwarf nandina, flowering pomegranate, lilac, and zygocactus. Tags and posted information are pretty minimal, but communication with the folks who run this interesting place is worth establishing.

MERLOT NURSERY
701 North Gate Road
Walnut Creek
(510) 943-1958
FAX (510) 943-2386
Daily 8 A.M.–5 P.M.
Wheelchair accessible

A recent start on the site of—and coexisting with—a working hobby vine-yard, Merlot specializes in drought-tolerant plants. In particular there are lots of trees, both natives and exotics, in several sizes at good prices, and evidently well cared for; also, an impressive variety of rosemary cultivars. Among the nondroughty specimens are fruit trees, shade trees like *Liriodendron* (tulip tree), small shade lovers like dogwood, and understory ferns, hostas, woodland flowers, and such, good for making an oasis in a dry spot. And, of course, Merlot sells grapevines of several sorts. Free local delivery.

SIMON HOME CENTER

1500 Botelho Drive
Walnut Creek
(510) 935-8100
Monday and Friday 9 A.M.–8 P.M. Tuesday–Thursday 9 A.M.–6 P.M.
Saturday 9 A.M.–6 P.M. Sunday 10 A.M.–5 P.M.
Wheelchair accessible

A great big hardware-and-accessories store that does a good job on its garden stuff. The nursery isn't huge, but has an interesting variety of plants, including things like Matilija poppy and California coffeeberry that you don't see everywhere, ceanothus trained up to standards, cacti and succulents, and very inexpensive one-gallon shrubs. Information tags are quite well done, and staffers are friendly, thorough, informative, and efficient. The edibles are routine but cheap. A section of inexpensive, healthy-looking houseplants includes some large and interesting specimens.

The tool selection's good, too, and includes bonsai tools and things as useful and whimsical as really sturdy fuchsia-colored leather garden gloves. For bonsai, you can also find good containers, including those big brown drum pots. Lots of regular containers, boxes, and pots, too; some unusual trellises, fencing, prefab gates; pavers and retaining-wall blocks (given a handsome demonstration site in the parking lot); doghouses and birdbaths and -feeders for your nonhuman allies; and furniture including pieces made of wicker, resin, or wood, or metal and glass. Some, like a rather handsome sling chair, are sized for small spaces.

NORTH BAY

HORSESHOE HILL NURSERY

190 Horseshoe Hill Road
Bolinas
(415) 868-2539
Allegedly open Sundays only
Wheelchair accessible

If you happen to stumble upon this one when it's open (Sundays and by appointment; aside from the day, hours are not posted), you might find something you didn't know you wanted. The small stock consists mostly of fairly unusual perennials, including some small sizes and border plants. The plantings that greet you in the tiny parking lot are inspiring enough for a second look. You can buy some bagged soil amendments and planting mix here, too.

LARNER SEEDS

235 Grove Road
Bolinas
(415) 868-9407
Tuesday 10 A.M.–1 P.M. Saturday noon–3 P.M.

This is a nursery with a mission—actually, the mission came first. Larner's proprietor Judith Lowry is a native-plant fan who has been growing for seeds since 1977, and is heavily involved in restoration gardening. She does design and planting consultations for those who want to restore their own yards and preserve displaced species. Larner Seeds are found in the best nurseries, and at California Native Plant Society sales; here you can buy seeds *and* plants grown from them.

LAS BAULINES NURSERY

Bolinas Road
Bolinas
(415) 868-0808
Daily 10 A.M.–5 P.M.
Wheelchair accessible, mostly, if your chair is narrow and you're athletic. The
ground is rough, some deeply mulched areas and slopes.

Strategically situated between the obligate birders' stop at the mouth of Pine
Gulch Creek and the lunch stop in downtown Bolinas, this nursery is of the
small but choice variety. Fruit trees, for example: there aren't glades of them,
but they are unusual—greengage plum, 'Winter Banana' apple—and chosen with an eye for the local climate. Information tags are spotty, but useful
when they exist; the place is small enough and its workers approachable
enough that you might not need tags at all. There are things like billbergia,
gunnera, Hankow willow, several sorts of palm and bamboo, grasses and succulents of enough variety that you have a good chance of seeing something
new, too. Herbs include medicinals. Edibles, again, are chosen to suit the
climate: things like cherry tomatoes, seed potatoes, greens. You can do a surprising amount of rambling in this small place, through the shade house,
around the herbs, out the back to where the stock blends almost seamlessly
with the pond and the wild background. In the shop, you can find indoor
plants, including some impressively tall orchids; cut flowers; containers;
cover-crop seeds; Larner Seeds and Shepherd's Garden Seeds; less-toxic pest
controls; and organic supplements sold by the scoop.

HAWAIIAN TROPICALS BONSAI

1858 Redwood Highway
Corte Madera
(415) 924-7633
Monday–Friday 10 A.M.–9 P.M. Saturday 10 A.M.–7:30 P.M. Sunday 11 A.M.–6 P.M.
Wheelchair accessible, but a tiny space. It's all easily visible from the
entrance; basically it's a glass booth.

It's a mall—The Village at Corte Madera—and they're mall bonsai. The only
thing even a little tropical-looking I've seen there was a sago palm, which is

not exactly Hawai'ian. There are small-leaved tropical species, like serissa, which isn't Hawai'ian either. Trees only, no equipment; prices are pricey; one of these might make a good gift, but a single good class and a gallon-size sapling would be a better investment in bonsai. That said, what I've seen here has been good, for the genre, and includes some species that can survive indoors.

NURSERY AT FAIRFAX LUMBER
109 Broadway
Fairfax
(415) 453-4410
Monday–Friday 7:30 A.M.–6 P.M. Saturday and Sunday 8:30 A.M.–5 P.M.
Wheelchair accessible

Like most nurseries appended to hardware and lumber stores, this one will give you lots of the basics. Its strengths lie in water and pond plants, kits, and equipment; some interesting trees, including fruit trees and palms; berries and vines; and shade-lovers including ferns and tree ferns. Lots of good containers in many sizes and styles. You can get tools, lumber, and hardware here, too, of course, so if you're building your frogs a hot tub, it's one-stop shopping. Staff are attentive and pretty knowledgeable, and the information tags are systematic and useful.

O'DONNELL'S FAIRFAX NURSERY
1700 Sir Francis Drake Boulevard
Fairfax
(415) 453-0372
Daily 9 A.M.–5:30 P.M.
Wheelchair accessible, if you're fairly athletic and maneuverable.

That outsize turtle that greets you as you thread your way into O'Donnell's is a functional worm-composting box, and about typical of the attitude here — no, not slow and crawly: down-to-earth, smart, and a little outrageous. O'Donnell's emphasizes two things that won me over fast: organically raised plants and California natives. There are interesting edibles, including heirloom tomatoes in season; perennials and shrubs, including antique roses; color and trees and prime examples of all the expected goodies; tools, soil amendments, less-toxic pesticides, some ornaments. But the real head-turners here are the California plants, in particular the native trees. I've seen species here that usually turn up in California Native Plant Society sales and almost nowhere else: desert willow with its fragrant flowers, Jeffrey pine, native alder, Sitka spruce, toyon. Smaller natives include several species and varieties of *Sisyrinchium* (blue-eyed or yellow-eyed grass, a tiny iris relative), and many other surprises. The owners and staff here know their materials, too, and the informal, zesty atmosphere invites the sharing of information and ideas.

HOUSEPLANT MARKET
2040 Redwood Highway
Larkspur
(415) 924-8410
Monday–Friday 10 A.M.–9 P.M. Saturday 10 A.M.–8 P.M. Sunday 10 A.M.–7 P.M.
Wheelchair accessible

Attached to a Cost Plus, this is a good source for houseplants at off hours, since it keeps the same hours as the import store. A reasonable range of houseplants including orchids and big palms, ficuses, dracaenas, and such; containers, flower-arranging equipment and materials, the odd hand tool, and plant food.

GREEN GULCH FARM
Route 1, south of Muir Beach
(415) 383-3134
Daily 9 A.M.–noon, 1:30 P.M.–4 P.M.
Wheelchair accessible; can be strenuous, depending
on where you can park.

This is a relaxing place to visit, once you find the garden. The roadlet from Route 1 is paved but not wide, and requires civilized driving behavior especially if you meet a van coming the other way. The driveway leads to a parking lot, where there's a $5 parking fee on Sundays between 8:45 and 10:30 A.M. (unless you have three or more people in your car; then it's free) because of the zazen and lectures scheduled then. Parking on Route 1 and walking down the driveway isn't a good option, either, since there's no shoulder and it's a busy highway. Once you're at the visitor lot, you still have a stroll ahead, and it's decidedly pleasant, past a lively pond, through some conifer forest and a scatter of variously stylish and improvised buildings; take the path to the right of the lawn past the office and descend to the garden gate. Here is the image of peaceful prosperity: birds venture close and there are coveys of quail despite the several cats wandering around; cordoned fruit trees separate thriving beds of vegetables and flowers; there are several garden "rooms" marked off by tall conifer hedges in a decidedly European style and enclosing benches, a birdbath or two, a statue adorned with bright necklaces. The sales section is between these and the larger row-crop garden. You'll find gallon perennials at good prices, occasionally some larger perennials, and old-fashioned roses. There are tables of culinary, medicinal, and tea herbs, a shrub or two; the stock here is clearly seasonally tidal. In season, you can get vegetable seedlings for a quarter. The information tags are clearly the work of a devoted gardener; each contains the plant's name, its uses, habits, looks, and preferences, and often how it is propagated. All are raised organically. Who knows? That, or the general peaceable ideology, may explain the trees and sky full of birds—Swainson's thrush, warblers, phoebes and flycatchers, blackbirds, chickadees, jays, hawks, and more—and the parking lot full of bunny rabbits. Green Gulch hosts classes regularly, with guest and staff teachers, and has a volunteer gardening program Tuesday, Thursday, and Saturday from 9 A.M. to noon. Volunteers are invited to stay for lunch, and asked to call the office number above before coming to work.

CALIFORNIA BAY NURSERIES
399 Entrada Drive
Novato
(415) 883-6383
Daily 8:30 A.M.–5:30 P.M.
Wheelchair accessible

On the small side of moderately sized, California Bay is strongest on quick color, including instant-gratification perennials like pelargoniums; edibles including grapes, citrus varieties, and veggie notables, some organically raised, such as rhubarb; and heat-tolerant shade trees—I saw two kinds of cassia there. With patience, you might start your own spice plantation. The small staff answers questions intelligently, and California Bay offers free design help. There are tools, soil amendments, fertilizers, and pesticides; a good group of indoor plants, and a growing number of interesting containers, worth checking out.

FLOWER POWER

11275 State Route 1
Point Reyes Station
(415) 663-8221
FAX (415) 663-8544
Daily 10 A.M.–"5ish" P.M.

Not a lot of plants in this little shop's backyard, but the ones that are there are tempting: old roses, herbs, shrubs, perennials, a few veggie starts. Inside and out are ornaments, wind chimes, pots, baskets, hooks and hangers, birdfeeders and birdhouses, decorative watering cans, hand tools, less-toxic pest controls, plant foods, and gopher baskets. You can pick up a pair of earrings and a skirt for your garden party, too.

Just down the street, at 11315 Route 1, the Brown Study Bookshop offers quite a respectable few shelves of antique and plain old old gardening books, and sometimes used issues of *Pacific Horticulture* magazine. It's open 10 A.M. to 5 P.M. Friday through Monday "and the rest of the week, by chance." Call (415) 663-1633.

TOBY'S FEED BARN

Route 1
Point Reyes Station
Monday–Saturday 9 A.M.–5 P.M. Sunday 9:30 A.M.–4:30 P.M.
Wheelchair accessible

There's a small but effective selection of perennials arranged outside Toby's barn door, and other items of interest to gardeners inside: Larner and Territorial Seed Company seeds and catalogs, good terra-cotta pots, ornaments, wind chimes, birdhouses, birdfeeders and seed, cover-crop seed, outdoor furniture, tools, pesticides, *Garden Design* magazine, and, for the really complete garden, pig chow.

NATURAL GARDENING COMPANY

217 San Anselmo Avenue
San Anselmo
(415) 456-5060
Catalog: (707) 766-9303
Catalog FAX (707) 766-9747
Monday–Saturday 9:30 A.M.–5:30 P.M. Sunday 10 A.M.–5 P.M.

When you need a Thistle Monster or a tomato you never heard of, here's where to go. Actually, you don't have to go; Natural Gardening does catalog sales, too. But it's more fun to walk into Tomato Heaven (a trademarked epithet, and you can get a hat or T-shirt to prove it) and inhale the fragrance of the culinary herbs, peppers, greens, strawberries, lavender, and posies, all grown organically, all at least a little unusual. That's true of the tools, too—the thistle thing is a sort of giant pliers; there are more variations on the hoe and the hand weeder here than you might imagine possible, and Natural Gardening was the first kid on the block with that elegant spiral tomato support. They sell serious irrigation tools and equipment here, too, even line-cleaning tools for people who irrigate with silty well water, as well as water-conservation guru Robert Kourik's kits and book; they'll give you free system design help, too. Composters, compost, soil amendments and supplements, landscape fabrics, garden furniture—a little of everything, and all of it cleverly designed and chosen. This is what Smith & Hawken would be with less money and more dirt on its hands.

Sonoma County's nurseries are a book in themselves, and indispensable to Bay Area gardeners. One of my favored day trips through Sonoma's nurseries and other nice places follows a course like this:

Take Route 101 north to the Route 116 West exit, between Cotati and Rohnert Park. As soon as you hit Terra Noninterstate, you'll be presented with a set of nurseries to browse through, starting right at the exit with the **Windmill Nursery.** The Windmill is colorful and inviting, and not a bad place to look for water plants. (Ingenuity, and maybe an ice chest that doesn't leak, may be called for to get these home. I recommend the ice chest even if you get the plants in leakproof bags; there's some twisty road ahead, and peace of mind is a wonderful thing.) Along 116, you also have the options of **Sumagama's Nursery** (whose marquee promises "BIZARRE UNUSUAL FANTASTIC") and several others, a little funkier in feel than Windmill and with a high probability of surprises. In particular, look for bonsai material and four-inch perennials. There are lots of stops on the road before Sebastopol: other nurseries like **Koala-T Orchids** (I passed this place three times, attending to my driving like a good citizen, before realizing it was an orchid nursery and not an Australian stuffed toy shop), and antiques, crafts, produce, and local-color stores. Residents along this and other Sonoma country roads sometimes sell plants and craft items out of their homes, so keep a left eye out for garage sale signs. It helps to have a farsighted copilot.

You might take Lone Pine Road, a left turn just after Hessel Road, to **Lone Pine Gardens,** at 6450 Lone Pine Road, the source for most of the bonsai babies in Bay Area nurseries, and a good place for herbs, unusual tree seedlings, and odd succulents, too. Then backtrack to 116. In Sebastopol, turn left onto the Bodega Highway, Route 12, west toward Bodega; turn right onto the Bohemian Highway at Freestone, and take a look at the **Wishing Well Nursery.** Then onward toward Bohemia. This will take you through Occidental, a town that seems devoted entirely to food. My kind of town.

In the middle of Occidental, turn left onto Coleman Valley Road, and take that to **Western Hills Nursery** at 16250 Coleman Valley. It's open Thursday through Sunday from 10 A.M. to 4 P.M. in the warm months; in midwinter—January, February—call before you set out, because the folks here open then only by appointment. The number's (707) 874-3731. There are some slightly intimidating signs at the garden gate about keeping small fry under close control and not expecting picnic facilities, but as is often the case, the people here are perfectly friendly and engaging to anyone acting reasonably, including children. As for picnicking, there's hardly room to turn around here, let alone sit down with lunch. You won't mind. This garden is enough to make you forget any other appetite for a while.

At first glance, it may look like an exercise in putting as many disparate plants as possible as close together as possible, but the effect is extraordinarily pleasing, and the reason for that becomes clear as you stroll, pause, and wriggle through the winding paths. This arrangement is not random or accidental, though I suspect some of it is integrally instinctive, as good art is. Views are planned, contrasts are honored, themes are carried out with various subtleties and echoes and the occasional exclamation point. And the plants! Take your time, and you'll want to take notes as well; there are more exotic (and native), differently gorgeous, striking, and harmonizing species and varieties here than in the average botanical garden. Western Hills has an advantage over official bot gardens in one respect: plants here aren't chosen or laid out for ease of study or the display of species' characteristics, but purely for art's sake. Plants are grouped together because they work together, physiologically and aesthetically. A gardener can study this garden for nonscientific reasons entirely, and apply ideas at home freely.

And you'll want to. There are things here even a Zen gardener can use. And here's the best and most dangerous part: you can buy a lot of it. There are hundreds of four-inch and gallon perennials, and a few trees in both those sizes, mostly alphabetized, and pretty well labeled, for sale in the nursery. Staffers are solicitous and informed; a "What's *this*?" will get a quick answer and often a good story, too. There's not an ordinary or dull plant in the lot, either. It will take great restraint not to spend the family fortune on plants here.

After you stagger out of Western Hills, take Coleman Valley Road back into Occidental, turn left, and then right almost immediately at Graton Road. Go through Graton, cross 116, and you'll find the name of the road you're on is now Frei Road. At Guerneville Road, take a little jog left and then right, so you've crossed Guerneville and are now heading north on Trenton-Healdsburg Road. Follow the signs for the Mark West Winery. You might want to stop at the winery for a taste or two of their nice product to brace yourself for the find in their backyard. The greenhouse behind the tasting room is the home of **California Carnivores**.

Peter D'Amato clearly has fun with the faintly sinister air that conventional wisdom gives these insect- (and sometimes small vertebrate-) eating plants. The greenhouse is festooned with rubber snakes, spiders, skeletons, and assorted kid-ghoulish decor, and at least one cultivar is named "Abandon Hope." (The Dantean imperative hangs over the hothouse door, too.) The sales table is in the center; around the walls of the greenhouse are specimens of some of nature's oddest-looking as well as oddest-behaving children. Venus's-flytraps, cobra lily (that's our own native *Darlingtonia*, denizen of cool-water bogs near the northern coast and in the mountains), pitcher plants of several sorts, and *Nepenthes*, whose rococo-condom traps are held determinedly upright on the ends of long, dangling stems. If you buy a few of these plants, ask about what they like; you'll have much better luck in keeping them alive if their relatively simple but unusual desires are fulfilled. Everything has an information tag that spells out whether it should live indoors or out, needs a winter dormant period, or has other quirks.

Back to Trenton-Healdsburg Road for a short stretch. Another of those left-right jogs at Mark West Station Road puts you on Eastside Road, where you'll find **Ya-Ka-Ama Nursery**. Follow the road to the Youth Authority's facility, and look to your right for the arrow (a realistic arrow, which may be otherwise unlabeled) that points the way to the nursery and cultural center. The official address is 6215 Eastside Road, Forestville; phone is (707) 887-1586. This one is more likely to be open for business on a weekday; on weekends, there will ordinarily be little activity, but there's a resident caretaker there who will sell you a plant or two if you have the exact change in cash. The demonstration herb garden, under reconstruction at press time, is worth a look. Ya-Ka-Ama means "Our Land." This is a nursery run by Native Californians (most of the people I've met there are Miwok) that concentrates on native California plants, with a strong sideline of useful herbs. Prices are good, and you can learn a thing or two about what plants are used for in traditional Californian cultures.

Turn back down Eastside the way you came, and turn left (east) on River Road. That will take you to Fulton, where a right on Somers Street will put you at **California Flora Nursery**, at Somers and D Streets. Summer hours are Monday through Friday 9 A.M. to 5 P.M., Saturday and Sunday

10 A.M. to 4 P.M.; winter hours, Monday through Friday 10 A.M. to 4 P.M., closed weekends. You can call them at (707) 528-8813. It's an engaging small nursery with an excellent stock of perennials, herbs, shrubs, and trees, many of them California natives. A typical price list includes twelve kinds of ceanothus. A major shade structure here is a well-inhabited old oak, whose presence seems to have blessed the place.

A right turn back onto River Road, a couple of blocks to the freeway again, and you can take your prizes and the day's sights home. If you've picked up a Farm Trails map at one of your stops, you'll see that this is only the beginning of Sonoma's possibilities.

RED HILL NURSERY
836 Sir Francis Drake Boulevard
San Anselmo
(415) 455-8350
Daily "8 or 8:30 A.M.–7 or 7:30 P.M."
Wheelchair accessible; tight spaces.

If the hours sound vague, well, this is Marin. (Note the late closing hour for a nursery, though.) You didn't think you'd get through this whole book without a Marin joke, did you? You can buy crystals here, too, along with other ornamental stuff, and containers, tools, handy chemicals, seeds, and bulbs. The plant selection is concentrated—in fact, the whole nursery is concentrated, tucked into a sliver of the Red Hill shopping center. There are roses (and a "rose hospital," where you can leave potted patients to be treated), interesting perennials, and large quick-color plants; shade trees; a small group of edibles; vines and shrubs; a good selection of shade-loving stuff. If you don't see what you want, or don't know what you want, ask; Red Hill specializes in service, including special orders, and the owner/manager is cheerfully ready with (from what I've overheard) accurate advice. I have to congratulate him on the clever water recycling system, which takes advantage of the fully paved space and involves an underground cistern and a fertilizer mixer. Plants in containers can have their roots fried by sitting on sun-heated asphalt, but the stock here looks happy and healthy; the system, and careful attention, allows them all the water they need without running up outrageous bills.

SUNNYSIDE NURSERY
130 Sir Francis Drake Boulevard
San Anselmo
(415) 453-2701
Daily 8:30 A.M.–5 P.M.
Wheelchair accessible but space is very tight.

A fair-sized nursery crammed into a small space and set up in an arrangement that works as a maze, leading customers on a short nature walk to a creek out back. Particular strengths here are shade-lovers, including Japanese maples, which are thoroughly described on information tags and a wall chart complete with spring, fall, and winter colors. These people are serious about giving you exactly what you want in a Japanese maple, and they stock enough of them to do that. Other trees include an interesting assortment of fruits, good on the citrus particularly—I suppose if you're going to get a 'Buddha's Hand' citron to thrive anywhere in Marin, this warm inland side of the mountain is the place, and Sunnyside is optimistic enough to sell them. Information posting in general is quite good here, a good idea in a small nursery with a small staff and a large clientele. There are lots of ornamentals, vines, shrubs, perennials, and color; a fair selection of veggies and herbs; good tools including bonsai tools; some very handsome pots and containers; ornaments including a multicultural pantheon of statues; the usual soil amendments and supplements, bagged; houseplants, not inexpensive but flourishing and including such distinctive specimens as *Raphis* palms among a good, wide range.

TANEM'S GARDEN CENTER
273 North San Pedro Road, San Rafael (415) 472-6121
1520 Tiburon Boulevard, Belvedere (415) 435-0041
Monday–Saturday 9 A.M.–5 P.M. Sunday 9:30 A.M.–4 P.M.
Wheelchair accessible

Bob Tanem's genial voice can be heard on KSFO radio on Sunday mornings, talking about gardening; here's where he walks his talk. His nurseries pay attention to such local niceties as microclimate and nonhuman neighbors, specializing in deer-resistant plants and offering a certain amount of expertise on this extremely unpredictable topic. He also experiments with less-toxic pest controls like oyster shell to repel snails, and has mostly the more benign sort of pesticide on his shelves. The nurseries have a good stock of perennials, color, shrubs, and trees, particularly Japanese maples.

TERRA LINDA NURSERY
636 Freitas Parkway
San Rafael
(415) 472-1730
Tuesday–Sunday 9 A.M.–6 P.M. Closed Monday

On a skinny site that looks best suited for a spaghetti farm, Stephen Kling is working on a community-oriented nursery. He stocks some interesting trees and shrubs, including California natives (I found a native hazelnut here, and I don't see those for sale often) and fruit trees. One can't stuff great numbers of plants into this roadside sliver, so they've been chosen with care; there are plants you'll see elsewhere, and unusual ones, too, clearly chosen with an eye to the microclimates: peanuts and okra among the edible seedlings, for the hot side of Marin; grasses, succulents, and other perennials; and shade-garden things like Japanese and moon maples, ferns, indoor specialties. There are a few ornaments and tools, and small water-garden containers. Good personal information supplements the fair information tags. There's also work from local artists on the walls, a community bulletin board, and a place to sit and have coffee and pastries in the shade.

UNITED MARKETS NURSERIES
515 Third Street
San Rafael
(415) 454-8915
Monday–Saturday 9 A.M.–6 P.M. Sunday 9 A.M.–5:30 P.M.
Wheelchair accessible

A small nursery, maybe the logical extension of the market's fresh produce department. Procrastinators like me can get gallon-size tomatoes to plant; there are some fruit trees, including citrus; a pretty big selection of big ferns and other shade-lovers; perennials and annuals and nice gallon-size quick color; a handful of houseplants at good prices. Information tags are good. Containers range from half barrels to some rather ornate pottery.

WEST END NURSERY
1938 Fifth Avenue
San Rafael
(415) 454-4175
Monday, Tuesday, Thursday–Saturday 8 A.M.–5 P.M. Sunday 9 A.M.–3 P.M.
Closed Wednesday
Wheelchair accessible

Good array of trees, including carob, catalpa, redbud, and a Myoporum carsonii labeled "sandalwood" (it's really a congener of something called "bastard sandalwood"). Fruits include large citrus, grapes, raspberries, gooseberries, and kiwis. Other edibles I've seen here aren't rare, but are chosen with the local conditions in mind. Shrubs include some decent natives; there are perennials, vines, and bedders, too, along with an impressive lot of pots.

MERISTEM/STINSON BEACH FLOWERS
3472 Shoreline Highway
Stinson Beach
(415) 868-0666
FAX (415) 868-2309
Wednesday–Sunday 10 A.M.–5 P.M.

A very small place with a lot packed into it, this one caters to the weekend-house-on-the-beach crowd with annual color and fast solutions, and manages to slip in a few treasures for the discerning and the adventurous besides: Catalina ironwood, ceanothus, and assorted nifty herbs and shrubs, chosen to thrive in the local microclimate. You can get cut flowers and cards, soil amendments and fertilizers and such, and some very intriguing containers and artifacts. There are some informational tags, but the place is so small they're almost redundant. You don't have to yell to be heard from the other side of the lot, and the owners/managers, who know their stuff, are interested in talking about it.

MOSTLY NATIVE NURSERY
Route 1
Tomales
(415) 878-2009
Monday, Wednesday–Saturday 9 A.M.–5 P.M. Sunday 11 A.M.–5 P.M. Closed
Tuesday
Wheelchair accessible

This one's a classic. It's a California native plant wholesale source for other nurseries, and I take it as a recommendation for the others that they get their natives here. Mostly Native's stock is a revelation: rare things like fawn lily and Sierra rose (I've seen three native rose species here), and merely unusual and handsome things like ninebark, ocean spray, and Douglas (as well as the more commonly found Pacific Coast Hybrid) iris. There are more species of native bunchgrass than you can shake a stick at, and they're available as gallon-size or four-inch plants. Native shrub youngsters are here in four-inch sizes, too, to stretch your dollar and allow flexibility in use. These people clearly know what they're doing; the stock is dazzlingly healthy, questions get answers, and the informational tags are a horticulture course in themselves, with details like which plants are native to the Bay Area, what their cultural preferences are, what they'll tolerate, and which ones do well in containers.

"Mostly" isn't misleading, either; there are other plants here, a small but choice assortment, and as robust and inviting as the natives. Herbs include classics like lemon balm, and slightly adventurous things like Thai basil; the edibles are the sort of thing you want if you have precious little dirt space to squander. Prices are good for natives and exotics both. You can get soil amendments here, too, if you can resist spending your whole budget on plants.

PENINSULA

TYLER'S CARLMONT NURSERY
2029 Ralston Avenue
Belmont
(650) 591-6845
Daily 8:30 A.M.–5:30 P.M. April 1–June 15 8:30 A.M.–6:30 P.M.
Partly wheelchair accessible, approaching from the street side rather than
the shopping-center parking lot. Very steep and narrow paths to terraced
areas, and the shop isn't inviting to a wheelchair.

Tucked almost invisibly (from the parking lot) into a shopping center, this
fair-sized nursery is a study in space use. It rambles up and down and around
its limited square footage crammed with handsome trees, particularly Japanese and California vine maples—the latter is not easy to find in nurseries;
perennials, some unusual; a healthy stock of the usual annual color, again with
a few out of the ordinary; and edibles from fruiting white mulberry and a com-
paratively large assortment of avocados to kiwi vine and rhubarb, and the
more common stuff like greens and tomatoes. Somebody here likes fuchsias;
there are hangers, shrubs, and standards. There are David Austin roses, small
bonsai starts from Lone Pine and mall bonsai, and houseplants including some
very inexpensive small ones. Also on hand is a modest collection of pots and
containers, ornaments like wire topiary forms, hand tools, half-barrels, and
plant foods and chemicals including such handy stuff as antifruiting spray.
Staff are friendly and helpful even on a busy day. Carlmont publishes a pretty
good newsletter that includes recipes and an amusing incentive for reading:
one subscriber's name shows up in the text each month, and that subscriber
can spot the name and come in for a $20 gift certificate during the month.
It's free; add your name to the mailing list at the counter. The most striking
feature of the place is a humanmade creek rushing through it, over naturalistic cascades and meanders, that salutes the real creek that's culverted
underneath. This is the sort of thing that makes living in the twentieth
century so very odd.

BURLINGAME GARDEN CENTER

1427 Chapin Avenue
Burlingame
(650) 344-2539
Monday–Saturday 7:30 A.M.–3:30 P.M.
Wheelchair access limited to ground-level main display area.

A dressy example of concentrated gardening and use of tight spaces, this nursery rambles up and over a pair of rooftops and around corners of a small, airy lot. Along with healthy standards, you'll find Annie's Annuals; some slightly unusual herbs and veggies (Greek oregano, Chinese 'Ruby Pearl' tomatoes), and scented geraniums; lots of vines and shrubs trained to a standard for tight spaces; hanging plants and some citrus; also good hand tools, Birkenstock garden clogs, rain gauges, and other equipment. An interior collection with a high frou-frou quotient includes some inspiring orchids and other good houseplants. Tags, even price tags, are spotty, but staff are easy to talk to and helpful; it's the sort of place where clients bring in cuttings from sick plants and get quick advice and reassurance.

BLOOMING DALE'S NURSERY

1692 Old Mission Road
Colma
No phone listed. Very mysterious.
The plant and soil amendment areas are wheelchair accessible; the shop (tools and useful chemicals) is a trailer with steps.

What I'd come here for wasn't so much the plant stock, which looks a bit dispirited, but bulk soils, amendments, gravel, and bark chips, which you can haul or have delivered. Keep an eye out for bargains of the runt-puppy sort, and for the birds that frequent the place; what is it about nurseries that attracts red-shouldered hawks? There are hand tools, fertilizers and other handy ingredients, too, and parts for irrigation setups.

ALEC NURSERY
Hill and B Streets
Daly City
(650) 992-8462
Daily 9 A.M.–5:30 P.M.
Wheelchair accessible

This small neighborhood nursery carries mostly garden stalwarts (including broom, alas) with such variants as a grafted dwarf pink variegated lemon, and similar interesting dwarf citrus. There are edibles, with a slant toward things that will do well in the microclimate (collards, cherry tomatoes); in fact, a lot of the stock is clearly chosen with fog and wind in mind. On a first visit I wondered about a big tag on the *Arbutus unedo* that proclaimed it native to Ireland; overhearing the manager's comprehensive and friendly advice to a couple of customers clarified that the claim was a case of patriotism. They're cheerful about special orders here, if you should want something really unusual. Besides plants and good advice, you can get tools, basic containers, and fertilizers and such. The neatly handmade information tags make interesting reading, too.

BAYLANDS NURSERY
1165 Weeks Street
East Palo Alto
(650) 323-1645
Monday–Saturday 8 A.M.–4:30 P.M.
Wheelchair accessible; rough spots.

You can find your way here by the air traffic of one sort or another, as it lies adjacent to both the Palo Alto Baylands bird refuge and a small-craft airport. Among a lot of good, healthy, and interesting perennials, including things like francoas and striped-leaf iris, are Baylands' specialties: grasses, daylilies, and proteas. When the lilies are in flower the place is dazzling, and there are ranks and rows of them in the ground as well as in gallon cans. The grasses include varieties you don't see everywhere, and of course proteas are as unusual as they are Martian. (Strybing Arboretum has some good examples to look at.) Everything here is a perennial, a shrub, or a tree, and it's strictly plant stock, no tools or containers or such. There are a few succulents, some good California natives, grevilleas (which are odd enough to harmonize with proteas, heaven knows); some of the trees are large, twenty-four-inch boxed types. Not much in the way of labels, but the owner is there during open hours and he knows his stuff. In general the stock is various and inspired enough; you may feel all poetic and want to plant woodruff under your dogwood after shopping here.

BONGARD'S TREESCAPE NURSERY
12460 San Mateo Road (Route 92)
Half Moon Bay
(650) 726-4568
Daily 9 A.M.–5 P.M.
Wheelchair accessible; some spots are rough.

Treescape indeed: the big trees in twenty-gallon cans and even bigger ones in boxes are the most impressive things here, aside from the birds. (On a casual stroll through the place on a spring weekend, I saw or heard red-shouldered hawk, American goldfinch, warbling vireo, purple finch, Wilson's warbler, California quail, barn swallow, cliff swallow, the usual robin, Brewer's blackbird, turkey vulture, and a few more; I bet they have Swainson's thrush, too.) Distractions aside, once you manage to get into Bongard's tiny wedge of a parking lot without getting rear-ended, you'll find interesting trees and tree substitutes—things like tree ferns, and hopseed bush trained up to a standard. There are lots of shade plants like ferns and rhodies and clivias and fuchsias, a small assortment of one-gallon perennials and roses, and a jungle of vines and hanging plants in a greenhouse you'll be lured into by a long tunnel of jasmine and bougainvillea. A very few vegetable starts, and no tools, but some containers and that silly pelican sculpture you know you've always needed.

CAZZOLINO'S FLORIST AND NURSERY

12001 San Mateo Road (Route 92)
Half Moon Bay
(650) 726-4383
Monday–Saturday 7:30 A.M.–5 P.M. Sunday 9:30 A.M.–5:30 P.M.
Wheelchair accessible

There are a few surprises here, on the order of cork oak trees, white-flowering catmint, and blue *Cuphea* ("false heather"—one of several with that name), amid a great many healthy and good-looking standard offerings. Of course there are artichoke and pumpkin seedlings; this is Half Moon Bay. There are also rather a lot of poodle-balled and topiary shrubs, and a respectable assortment of perennials and roses, and quick-color annuals. No tools, just a few containers. Inside the greenhouse are lots of houseplants, including big showy specimens, and bromeliads and, again, a few surprises like carnivorous *Sarraceneas*. Cut flowers, too.

FLORA FARM NURSERY AND GARDEN SHOP

340 Purisima
Half Moon Bay
(650) 726-9223
Tuesday–Saturday 9 A.M.–5:50 P.M. Closed Sunday and Monday

Even on a closed day you may be greeted by a regal tortoiseshell cat hanging out with the cast-stone armadillos and the twig settee . . . well, it would be a settee if it weren't covered with ivy that it would not be sporting to sit on. So it must be art. The feel of the place is countrified-genteel, with rust-finish *tuteurs* and arches, cottagey four-inch perennials, and a barnboard building that may even have started out as a small barn. Flora sells sod, too, and other pedestrian necessities, and has an attached shop with wreaths and other indoor stuff.

A Gardener's Stroll through the Town of Half Moon Bay

It hasn't quite turned into Sausalito yet, but downtown Half Moon Bay is getting self-consciously touristy. They're handling it pretty well, though, and the Portuguese Pentecost celebration still exists as a civic endeavor along- side the more commercial Pumpkin Festival. The downtown shopping area is quaintly spiffy and it's possible to get a cheap and tasty sandwich there, as well as a Trendy Diner Breakfast. Gardeners will see pockets of inspira- tion. There are handsome little parks with tables or seating space, nicely planted, and private cottage gardens alongside antique stores and homes. A garden walkway between Main and Purisima Streets is a good example of how concrete and those clever devices for stamping it can make a good imitation of flagstone or brick paving, and of the joys of anal retentive lawn- and-border design.

There are several stores on or near Main Street that a gardener might find rewarding. Half Moon Bay Feed and Fuel (331 Main Street; Monday through Friday 9 A.M. to 6 P.M., Saturday 9 A.M. to 5 P.M., Sunday 10 A.M. to 4 P.M.) stocks pond equipment and preformed plastic liners, and goldfish to put in them; live traps for that pesky possum; tools including posthole dig- gers; sandbox sand; and birdhouses as well as Bag Balm for your hands when you're finished using the rest. You can get tack and custom-made chaps, too, if your gardening includes the larger sort of live ornament. Coastside Books at 521 Main Street has a small but lookworthy garden sec- tion, all new; Ocean Books across the street does, too, new and used. Half to Have It—The Main Street Exchange, at the corner of Main and Miramonte, is an antique store with a courtyard annex selling garden ornaments, step- ping stones, fountains, a few plants, and some attention-getting pots to put them in. It's open Sunday through Thursday 10 A.M. to 5 P.M., Friday and Saturday 10 A.M. to 6 P.M.

Unless you like car camping, by which I mean camping *in* your car, engine idling, on the road, in the company of several thousand others who are likewise ensnared, beware of the fall Pumpkin Festival weekend. The Festival itself can be fun, but Half Moon Bay's location at a bottleneck of Routes 92 and 1 makes the occasion a traffic nightmare. (If I sound bitter, it's because we've been caught in that nightmare while chasing an extral- imital bird down the coast, with pumpkins nowhere in mind.) Traffic gets infamously jammish on 92 on sunny weekends, too; if you can do your nurs- ery shopping on a weekday, you'll find it easier on the nerves. There are several nurseries and florists on 92, and they're good reasons not to tail- gate, as people are apt to do double takes followed by hair-raising turns into them. I've done it myself, and I know better.

HALF MOON BAY NURSERY
San Mateo Road (Route 92)
Half Moon Bay
(650) 726-5392
Daily 9 A.M.–5 P.M.
Wheelchair accessible; crowded and some tight spots.

This is Half Moon Bay's premier nursery. It even has its own SamTrans bus stop. Here you'll find banks of gorgeous and inexpensive fuchsias, handsome perennials in one-gallon and four-inch sizes, Annie's Annuals, a comprehensive assortment of herbs (including many varieties of mint and lavender, and two species of *Alchemilla*, lady's mantle), showy grasses, shrubs, bamboos, and more. The place is dizzying. These people don't stint on trees, either, with lots to choose from, including fairly unusual species like fernleaf Catalina ironwood and fringetree, and fruit varieties like 'Arkansas Black' apple. If you're shopping for shade trees, you may find yourself scurrying between here and Bongard's, just down the road, with a notebook in hand. There aren't any tools to speak of here, and only a few fertilizers, but there are lots of containers—red clay and white, glazed and not—and birdbaths, and a multicultural congregation of statuary.

GARDEN SUPPLY LOS ALTOS
4730 El Camino Real
Los Altos
(650) 948-2218
Monday–Friday 7 A.M.–6 P.M. Saturday 7 A.M.–5 P.M.
Wheelchair accessible

This is a second outpost of the Garden Supply company (the other one's in San Carlos); it sells about the same hardware, tools, features, and supplies and has more plants. Besides the usual suspects, it carries water and pondside plants, grasses, a few houseplants including palms, trees (some of them fairly unusual and some in twenty-four-inch box size), and lots of gallon perennials displayed alphabetically by Latin name.

LOS ALTOS NURSERY

245 Hawthorne Avenue
Los Altos
(408) 948-1421
Monday–Friday 9 A.M.–6 P.M. Saturday 8 A.M.–6 P.M. Sunday 9 A.M.–5 P.M.
Wheelchair accessible

Largish, dressy, and newly renovated, this nursery has been in this location and in the Furuichi family for some fifty years. It's a handsome setting for some very nice stock: lots of Japanese maples, abutilons, and other shade plants like ferns and fuchsias; Japanese-styled landscape pines, junipers, and cedars; a decent stock of edibles, including some interesting citrus like blood orange. There are some handsome, mostly formal pots and containers, SureFire nontoxic pest traps and some other less-toxic pest control substances, and a reasonable range of houseplants. There's an inspiring pond garden in front of the shop, with koi and water and waterside plants, and one of those funny little bridges that seem to exist to be stood on rather than crossed to anywhere. Staff are easygoing and helpful.

ALLIED ARTS GUILD

75 Arbor Road at Cambridge
Menlo Park
(650) 326-3632, information
(650) 324-2588, lunch reservations at the Allied Arts Restaurant
Monday–Saturday 10 A.M.–5 P.M.
Wheelchair accessible

Here's a special case: a public garden with retail shops, including a small, charming nursery with a choice collection of containers and ornaments. Nature's Alley, the nursery, whose phone number is (650) 326-3632, specializes in the extremely genteel: ivy topiaries, small container plants, wall plaques, fountains—mostly of the brimming-over rather than the expectorating variety—and trellises. The look runs mostly to the rustic-formal, with rust-finished, neatly formed iron pieces and elegant, simple shapes, some framing more elaborate decor. Nature's Alley has a couple of neighbors of particular interest to gardeners, too. Special Handling Pottery, (650) 321-8188, opens at 11 A.M., a little later than other shops here, and its wares include distinctive containers for plants and water gardens, some at very reasonable prices. At the end of the courtyard is the studio of Rob Browne, (650) 325-6832, where you'll be greeted by a sculpted hippo half-submerged in a gravel "pond." Browne makes other critters suitable for garden use: cats, dolphins, the odd space alien. If you're lucky, you might get a chance to talk with the personable artist himself; ask him about the gardens here, which he helps maintain.

These and a double handful of other shops are scattered in the corners and crannies and walks of a splendid set of gardens done in the Spanish style, with beautifully styled and chosen plants—the gardeners who maintain them more or less rotate between here and Filoli, and the Filoli training shows—and various degrees of formality. There are large open areas in the classic style, quartered by paths and focused on tiled fountains, and there are rustic little courtyards that might inspire imitation in warm areas. The paving is particularly interesting—it's concrete worked to duplicate the look of brick and tile and masonry. There's a brochure that tells the history and use of the place, which is run for the benefit of patients at Stanford's Packard Children's Hospital. It's an excellent place to stroll, study the artistry, and drop a little money for social benefit.

LADERA GARDEN CENTER
380 Ladera Country Shopper, on Alpine Road
Menlo Park
(650) 854-3850
Monday–Saturday 9 A.M.–6 P.M. Sunday 9 A.M.–5 P.M.
Wheelchair accessible; crowded inside and out.

This pleasant spot, tucked away in a shopping center closer to Portola Valley than to Menlo Park proper, has lots of quick-effect, long-lasting color like big pelargoniums, vines, and inexpensive four-inch perennials; a modest quantity of fruit trees including some different varieties like 'Anna' apples; some California natives suited to the warm spots, like woolly blue curls; standards like roses, Japanese maples, azaleas. Staff and owner are attentive and know the area as well as their plants, which is always an advantage. The front entrance is through a shop with quite a few houseplants, tools, soil amendments and such, and a lot of interesting containers, including big Malaysian pots; it also has fountains, ornaments, and knickknacks in a number of styles, from airport-exotic to old-fashioned tole. They sell Botanical Interests seeds, and such ingenious less-toxic pest controls as Garlic Barrier insect repellent.

ROGER REYNOLDS NURSERY AND CARRIAGE STOP
133 Encinal Avenue
Menlo Park
(650) 323-5612
Daily 9 A.M.–5:30 P.M.
Partly wheelchair accessible; the shop has steps.

"Why Carriage Stop?" I asked a random staffer. "Oh, we don't know really; that's just what Granny used to call it."

The Carriage Stop is the little shop of houseplants, gifts, baskets, and cachepots adjacent to the nursery shop. It was once a guest house on a circular drive, when the property this big dressy nursery stands on was the home of the family that still owns it. Several of the staff seem to be family—or at least familiars. There's good information on tags and signs all over, plus a staffed info booth with reference books and a place to read them. A different sort of information is available in the rear of the lot, which is a stroll garden with spots to sit and rest. Every plant in the garden is labeled and nicely placed, and it's all shaded by redwoods. It's quite an inviting spot and, I would think, makes the nursery a good neighbor to the apartment blocks ranged around it. Spread over the rest of the lot are such interesting things as outdoor bromeliads, water plants and a koi pool, shade trees and topiaries (including poodled pines, ouch), some unusual perennials in gallon and four-inch sizes, quick color and annuals, edibles including Upstarts organically raised seedlings, and mushroom-growing kits. There are bonsai starts, and mall-grade bonsai, with a few trees a cut above that, all healthy; and a decent selection of bonsai pots, wire, and tools.

Ornaments abound, most with a formal air: trellises, *tuteurs*, Italianate terra-cotta pots, bunnies and cherubs and the other usual pests, fountains and pond gear. In the main shop are hand tools, *Sunset* books, seeds including Botanical Interests and Seeds of Change, plant foods, pesticides, and soil amendments. Info tags in general are plentiful and thorough, always a good idea in a largish nursery; Reynolds also has classes, fruit tastings, and such every couple of months, and issues a newsletter.

PETERS AND WILSON NURSERY

11 Rollins Road
Millbrae
(650) 697-5373
Daily 9 A.M.–5:30 P.M.
Winter hours: Monday–Saturday 9 A.M.–5 P.M. Sunday 11 A.M.-4 P.M.
Wheelchair accessible

A great big nursery with a jet-plane chorus for entertainment, this place may be the antithesis of the serene country nursery, but it greens up its place in the flight path beautifully. It won my affection with its excellent staff-written newsletter, which includes recipes, good advice, horticultural news, and a minimum of advertising. The nursery stocks lots of trees, many large, including species like Japanese fern or umbrella pine (*Sciadopitys verticillata*), that you don't see often. There are other unusual plants like black bamboo, a great many fruit trees including multiple-graft (Swiss Army?) trees, water-garden plants, veggie starts, shade-lovers, perennials, vines—some already trellised—and plenty of the more usual stuff, too. Lots of nonplant items: containers, including some decent bonsai pots; banners, tools, gardening books and magazines, ornaments and planter baskets; useful compounds like fertilizer and coyote urine; worm-composting equipment; seeds including Shepherd's Garden Seeds. Classes happen here, too, including composting and gardening classes sponsored by the city of Millbrae.

GO NATIVE NURSERY/CYPRESS FLOWER FARM

333 Cypress Avenue
Moss Beach
(650) 728-2286 FAX (650) 728-3067
gonative@coastside.net

Wednesday–Sunday, noon–6 P.M. (May be closed on dark rainy winter evenings, and from mid-December through mid-January; call first if in doubt.) Wheelchair accessible

This one's a hybrid labor of love. Cypress Flower Farm offers houseplants, art, pots, gifts, and cut flowers. Go Native, as the name implies, grows and sells California native plants, perforce specializing in those that will do well near the ocean, in the fog and wind and salt air. I saw plants there that I rarely see outside the California Native Plant Society's sales. (There's also a resident pair of red-shouldered hawks that hunt from the roof—having them so near is a privilege and a sign of a well-run nursery, I'd say.) The place is owner-staffed; they know their stuff and are adventurous in experimenting with uses for their species; you'll find plants you wouldn't expect in hanging baskets and acting like houseplants. Common houseplants like piggyback plant and maidenhair fern are California natives; someone like these folks must've had the idea first.

If you want to see how your piggybacks or ferns really prefer to live, go visit Fern Canyon in Prairie Creek Redwoods State Park, up north. It'll make you rethink your ambitions, or your plumbing.

SHELLDANCE BROMELIAD AND ORCHID NURSERY
2000 Cabrillo Highway
Pacifica
(650) 355-4845
Weekends only, 10 A.M.–5 P.M.
Wheelchair accessible; greenhouse has almost impossibly tight aisles.

Of course you've always wanted your own indoor jungle. There are indoor and outdoor orchids, bromeliads, and tillandsias—"air plants"—for sale here, and even more just to see. The Spanish mosses are astonishing, and they're just background material. There are books, art, pots, vases, and good advice. Shelldance runs classes on orchid culture and about the rainforests that many of these spectacular plants come from. It's also a good place for a picnic— and you're invited—or a jaunt to take in the view. The nursery is at the entrance to Sweeney Ridge—look up for migrating hawks in the fall.

BARRON PARK NURSERY

3876 El Camino Real
Palo Alto
(650) 424-9466
Monday–Saturday 8:30 A.M.–8 P.M. Sunday 9 A.M.–6 P.M.
Wheelchair accessible

This one's basically a florist that's branched out a little into houseplants; it's good for Norfolk Island pines (which do well outdoors, too), orchids, succulents including Christmas cactus, a few bedding plants, and miniature roses. There are containers, too, including some elaborate glazed pots.

COMMON GROUND ORGANIC GARDEN SUPPLY

2225 El Camino Real
Palo Alto
(650) 328-6752
Tuesday–Sunday 10 A.M.–5 P.M. Closed Monday
Wheelchair accessible; tight spots.

Here's an oasis in the concrete, in a Palo Alto block that's mostly asphalt and motor traffic. High-quality spades and digging forks hang in the window, inviting a serious gardener with a craving for cutlery. Inside there's a whiff of soil amendments, an assortment of hand tools, worm-composting equipment (you can order worms, too), and seeds from prime sources like Seeds of Change, Shepherd's Garden Seeds, and Bountiful Gardens (the house brand, raised in Willits) as well as jars of seeds to be measured out and bought in bulk. This sort of place is the second-best way to get new or old and unusual varieties of edibles and other plants—the first-best being Auntie Ev from Ohio or the mad gardener down the street. Out back, in the tiny courtyard, are seedlings for equally unusual herbs and vegetables, organic fertilizers, and soil amendments. There's purely pretty stuff here, like Japanese windbells and wrapping paper, and lots of information: garden books and magazines, a reference library and space to sit and peruse it, videos for rent, and a bulletin board for pro gardeners, services, and products. Common Ground runs classes in spring and fall, and has plenty of expertise on tap at any time; it's part of Ecology Action, John Jeavons's evangelical organization for French Intensive Gardening (see page 76). The results speak well for the method.

GREEN WORLD NURSERY
2701 El Camino Real at Page Mill Road
Palo Alto
(650) 325-2067
FAX (408) 738-3110
Monday–Friday 9:30 A.M.–7 P.M. Saturday 10 A.M.–6 P.M. Sunday 10 A.M.–5 P.M.
Wheelchair accessible

Just up the street from Barron Park Nursery, and around the corner from Ken's Bonsai Gardens, this little place offers some serious houseplant bargains, particularly in things like out-of-bloom African violets. There's some big stuff here, too; every parlor needs a tree.

KEN'S BONSAI GARDENS
471 Page Mill Road
Palo Alto
(650) 325-4840
Daily 9:30 A.M.–5 P.M.
Wheelchair accessible, but very narrow aisles and high display tables.

Just off El Camino Real, this unprepossessing front guards some striking bonsai whose ages are numbered in centuries, according to their owner, as well as smaller, younger beginner's trees. Some of the senior trees are grafted— white pine on black, for example, and Shimpaku on California juniper—a technique that raises some eyebrows but is widely accepted. But others are more straightforward, like the breathtaking trident maple that greets visitors just inside the gate. Of course these are priced in the thousands of dollars, but there are more affordable trees to be had among the relative youngsters. Many of the senior trees are imported from Japan; so were some techniques for importing and raising them, by the current owner's father well over forty years ago. The place is smaller than some living rooms, but sells, as well as trees, bonsai pots, tools, and equipment.

AL'S NURSERY
900 Portola Road
Portola Valley
(650) 851-0206
Weekdays 8:30 A.M.–5 P.M. Saturday and Sunday 9 A.M.–5 P.M.
Closed Wednesdays
Wheelchair accessible

I'll admit to liking these family-run nurseries with the family house on the premises; they remind me of my own gardening passion, with things just sort of taking over. This one further panders to my kind by stocking a pretty good number of California natives and more types of fruits than you see just everywhere: pluots, figs, and kiwis, among others. Lots of gallon perennials, roses, shade trees (some fairly unusual), and color; accessories like bird, bat, and butterfly houses; Botanical Interests seeds; less-toxic pest controls including lacewings, trichogamma wasps, and beneficial nematodes; tools; amendments; fertilizers and other useful chemicals. Information tagging isn't bad, but more is to be had by asking a staffer, who will probably be family, too. There are a few features strictly for fun here: a giant working waterwheel and a set of swings ("Play at your own risk") presided over by a rather imposing, solemn rabbit in a hutch.

M AND M NURSERY
332 Woodside Road
Redwood City
(650) 366-4429
Monday–Friday 8 A.M.–5:30 P.M. Saturday 8 A.M.–5 P.M. Sunday 9 A.M.–5 P.M.
Wheelchair accessible

Not quite a farm, though there are the usual vegetable starts plus artichokes, a good array of fruit trees including mulberry, and a coop of resident chickens. Perennials include daylilies and the usual suspects; trees include a fair choice of Japanese maples, small palms, and fifteen-gallon shade trees, some of which have looked a little peaked on particularly hot days, but most in good shape. Good prices on gardenia, daphne, and similar shrubs, and interesting grasses in four-inch pots; also noninteresting grasses as sod rolls. There are tools, containers, and fertilizers and such, but not much information in the form of tags, and not much staff either, though the one person I've met here was approachable and informed. This is probably a place to go if you already know what you want.

REDWOOD CITY NURSERY
2760 El Camino Real
Redwood City
(650) 368-0357
Monday–Saturday 8:30 A.M.–5:30 P.M. Sunday 9 A.M.–5 P.M.
Wheelchair accessible; tight spots crowded with plants.

Here's a great place to go find a tree you've never heard of. The flourishing stock here includes such unusual beauties as *Michelia doltsopa* and some of its even more unusual relatives, chaste tree, and lots of other shade, flowering, and fruit trees, some of which are those handy four-way grafts. There are good perennials, too, including rock-garden specialties, ferns, and vines; grasses and grasslike things like New Zealand flax and blue-eyed grass (which isn't, of course). Someone here has a good eye for leaf shape and plant form. You'll find the other nursery basics—some containers, fertilizers—and lots of information, both posted all over and from smart and enthusiastic staff. It's a nice green refuge from El Camino; anyone on foot in the neighborhood ought to stop in just to inhale.

WEGMAN'S NURSERY
492 Woodside Road
Redwood City
(650) 368-5908
Monday–Saturday 8 A.M.–6 P.M. Sunday 8 A.M.–5 P.M.
Wheelchair accessible; interior area is crowded.

No costumed weimaraners, but there are lots of cats. This is a busy, rather dressy nursery, wedged in among motels and convenience stores on a trafficky street, with attentive staffers and information displays all over. Along with the basics like ground covers, color, and perennials, there are Annie's Annuals, some water plants, and a few California natives like Matilija poppy, manzanita, Western redbud, and ceanothus. Lots of trees, including citrus as outré as blood orange, and other fruit trees; there's a handy info board with theoretical harvest dates listed for most varieties. The basic veggies are here, plus heirloom tomatoes, artichokes, celery, horseradish, melons, and herbs. There's a good selection of big and small houseplants, too, and succulents including a few column cacti; tools, Birkenstock clogs, fertilizers and such; little rolls of fencing, prefab gates, and potting tables; compost bins, and containers for indoors and out. The place has been in the family for a couple of generations, and nonfamily workers seem pretty attached to it, too, always a good sign about how things are run.

GARDEN SUPPLY SAN CARLOS
803 Old County Road
San Carlos
(650) 595-1404
Monday–Saturday 7:30 A.M.–3:30 P.M. Closed Sunday
Wheelchair accessible

Note the early contractors' hours here. You'll find an assortment of the usual plants, but the focus is on hardscape: lumber, railroad ties, rocks, pavers (including turf blocks and other fairly fancy items), drainage and irrigation equipment, bricks, bulk gravel, chips and soil amendments, and deck hardware. Tools include all those nifty things for working with concrete and irrigation pipe, and carpentry niceties like chalklines. There are pond kits and equipment, nursery tags, tree posts and guys, and quite an extensive array of path and feature lighting; big sacks of grass seed, deck stain and wood preservatives—clearly a place to shop if you're starting from the ground up.

CENTRAL GARDEN CENTER
408 Ninth Avenue
San Mateo
(650) 340-8850
Daily 9 A.M.–5 P.M.
Wheelchair accessible

Quite citified, a mostly ornamental-plant source, in an oaky location that is a pleasure in itself. There are some edibles, like grapes and blueberries, and the usual herbs plus some nonstandards like *shiso*. The stock is snugged into a small lot and looks impressively lush and healthy, and includes some interesting variations on the nursery regulars like pelargonium and begonia. Things in general tend toward the standard, but a cut above; the annual color stuff includes Annie's Annuals, for example, and seeds include Botanical Interests. There are ornaments and fountains, including some suitable for indoor use, and a gift shop with some antiques and houseplants. Staff is easygoing and knowledgeable.

GOLDEN NURSERY
1122 Second Avenue
San Mateo
(650) 348-5525
Monday–Saturday 8 A.M.–5 P.M. Sunday 9 A.M.–4 P.M.
Wheelchair accessible, but very very tight spots.

Second Avenue does a little trick of disappearing and showing up again several times, and the generally good local atlas I use doesn't warn about this trick. This makes Golden Nursery a bit hard to find, but when you do find it, fetched up against the freeway, it's fairly rewarding. It's a good general nursery with lots of healthy stock, almost enough to absorb the ambient traffic roar—rhodies and roses (including *Rosa rugosa*), shrubs, perennials, and color. Trees include interesting things like a variegated willow; fruit trees (and bushes—I've seen at least four or five varieties of blueberry here); and Japanese maple varieties, some fairly esoteric and some that are pruned and shaped bonsai-style, but landscape-size. Good finds here include very small water plants, as well as more standard sizes; similarly, lots of miniature roses; unusual fruit varieties, including citrus like calamondin and Seville orange; bonsai starts, wire, tools, and a few pots. There are also Botanical Interests seeds, some nice wrought iron trellises and such at good prices, sod, herbs, the usual soil amendments and useful chemicals, hand tools, and good advice. The plants, particularly the roses, are accompanied by detailed information tags and placards, and more information is to be had from a single-page newsletter.

COUNTRY GARDEN CENTER

1000 El Camino Real
South San Francisco
(650) 583-8421
Monday–Saturday 9 A.M.–5 P.M. Sunday 10 A.M.–4 P.M.
Generally wheelchair accessible

A longtime family nursery, with a decent and sometimes unusual stock of edibles, including Japanese tomato varieties raised from seed every year. There are also bonsai starts and shapely trees, fruit trees, shrubs including lots of roses, color, and a good perennial stock. Bonsai tools, too, and knowledge-able advice.

FARWELL'S RHODODENDRON NURSERY

13040 Skyline Boulevard
Woodside
(650) 851-8812
Friday–Tuesday 10 A.M.–4 P.M. Closed Wednesday and Thursday
An off-road wheelchair might negotiate this one, but it has rough, steep, and twisty paths on a generally sloping lot.

This nursery looks even more like an oasis than most do, because it keeps its stock not in nursery cans or boxes, but in the ground. The effect in spring is paradisaical. Waist-high rhododendrons and azaleas bloom beneath their larger exemplars along meandering paths, all on a slope opened among the conifers and oaks to a Pacific view. When you buy a plant, your choice is dug up and root-balled in plastic; be ready to dig it a hole when you get home. No tools, no containers, no flats of instant color or kitchen herbs here, just glorious rhodies and azaleas.

Just south on Skyline, the King's Mountain Country Store sports a hand-some raised-bed garden, part contained by a rock wall and part in wood. It's inspiring to look at. The store is closed Monday and Tuesday, so your chances of getting a cold drink after your rhodie raid are slim until the weekend. But the garden is right out front and easily seen anytime.

YERBA BUENA NURSERY

19500 Skyline Boulevard
(650) 851-1668
Woodside
Daily 9 A.M.–5 P.M.
Wheelchair accessible; some slopes. Tearoom and restroom are accessible;
shop has a couple of narrow steps.

This nursery is a pilgrimage destination for lovers of California native plants, including the winding, well-maintained dirt road that leads from Skyline to its entrance. In spring, native irises, columbine, and prairie stars nod from the road-cut banks at eye level; California bay laurel and Douglas fir scent the air; and Swainson's thrush, black-headed grosbeak, and assorted vireos and flycatchers court and carry on just out of sight. The trip builds an anticipation that's beautifully answered on arrival at the nursery itself, with its chattering creek at the parking lot, welcoming garden sculptures for sale, and plants as far as you can see. The people who work here are well informed, even expert; Yerba Buena is a propagating nursery, and most of what you see is grown by them on the spot. A list of what they grow would fill this chapter. It's all meticulously identified and healthy, and gets shown off in a rambling demonstration garden named for Gerda Isenberg, the nursery's founder. There are a very few nonnatives, mostly ferns in the fern house just uphill from the Tea Terrace, which is open for drinks and pastry on weekends, or for catered high tea midweek by reservation. The terrace and the garden shop have a very country-European air; aside from amusing ornaments, the shop sells excellent books, most oriented toward California native gardening; Larner native seeds (including a house wildflower mix); gifts and posters.

SOUTH BAY

CACTUS UNLIMITED
21030 Garden Drive
Cupertino
(408) 257-1047
Call for hours
See Cactus Flat, also in this section—unrelated nurseries; same problem for
Wheelchair access.

What is it about succulents that turns previously normal folks into fanatics?
Maybe it's the plants' attitude, strangeness, and charm. Maybe it's just their
variety—there's surprisingly little overlap in the stock between Cactus
Unlimited and Cactus Flat, for example. Cactus Unlimited is another cactus
nursery that has taken over its owners' home and yard since its start in 1950,
rendering a guard dog unnecessary and weeding impossible, though that's
not much of a problem: there's scarcely room for a weed. The focus here
leans toward zygocacti (orchid cacti), stapelias, and bromeliads as well as cacti
and euphorbias. They grow more than 3,000 varieties here and on their
Mojave growing ground. Many have spectacular flowers; for $2.50, Cactus
Unlimited will mail you an illustrated catalogue. Mail-order might be safer
than dodging through this prickly warren, but not half so much fun.

YAMAGAMI'S NURSERY
1361 South Saratoga-Sunnyvale Road
Cupertino
(408) 252-3347
Monday–Thursday 9 A.M.–6:30 P.M. Friday–Sunday 8:30 A.M.–6:30 P.M.
Wheelchair accessible

A big, fairly dressy nursery, organized (with signed pedestrian entrance and
exit lanes) for lots of traffic, Yamagami's greets the shopper with a small room
of indoor plants and ornaments, some witty: I saw window boxes with the
windows built in, plainly for hanging on a wall. There are rarities and surprises among the extensive and flourishing stock, like plumeria and proteas,

interesting succulents, and relatively common shrubs like juniper and camellia in attention-getting topiary and standard shapes. A good selection of edibles includes Upstarts organics, lots of fruit variety including grapes and lingonberries, and herbs. There are perennials, roses, shrubs, and vines, including lots of bougainvilleas; mall-grade bonsai; pond plants and gear; the seeds include Shepherd's Garden Seeds and Kitazama Asian vegetable seeds. Informational tagging is well done, and staff seem to know their stuff; you can get answers at a central information booth, too. There are lots of ornaments, pots, and tools; if none of these is the perfect gift, you can get a gift certificate—or a consultation or design voucher—at the register.

A TO Z TREE NURSERY
14350 Winchester Boulevard
Los Gatos
(408) 374-7350
FAX (408) 374-0345
Monday–Saturday 7:30 A.M.–5 P.M. Sunday 8:30 A.M.–5 P.M.
Wheelchair accessible plant display area

It doesn't go on beyond Zebra, but the tree selection here is fairly complete, for the standard, most-used species. This includes flowering, shade, and conifer varieties, all carefully labeled, and the trees here are big: fifteen-gallon cans to big twenty-four- and thirty-six-inch boxes. There are annuals and perennials, too, again from a standard palette, very reasonably priced. The place has an industrial wholesale feeling, probably in part because of the big-noise bustle of forklifts and front-loaders moving orders of bulk soils, amendments, gravel, sand, and rocks of all sizes from cobble to boulder, and because of the snaky stacks of drainage and irrigation tubing. The fast and systematic service is the best feature of the industrial atmosphere. There's a shade house with some nice tropicals and treeferns, incongruous in all the dust and diesel; in the office-shop you'll find tools, weed cloth, grass seed, fertilizers, pesticides, drip equipment, and popcorn. Popcorn? Coffee, too.

These folks will take back plastic nursery cans for reuse, and they give a deposit refund for five-gallon and larger sizes. They also run a hydroseeding operation, for those really difficult spots.

In association with its nursery operation, A to Z has two other specialized services :

TREE MOVERS
2190 Crittenden Lane
Mountain View
(415) 968-6117
FAX (415) 968-0171

What this sort of outfit does (there are others around) is remove great big
trees intact from one place and replant them in another, using a tree spade,
which is an enormous, complicated piece of machinery that I'd be tempted
to pay money just to see in action. When you're desperate for shade and a
great, green Presence, you call these folks and hope for a matchmaking with
someone who needs to add a wing to the house, or is plotting a subdivision;
otherwise, they'll deliver a tree from . . .

HILLSIDE FARMS
9401 East Road
Potter Valley
(707) 743-1674

This division grows big specimen trees, from four-footers to twenty-five-
and-up, of a relatively few species; the list includes such serious stuff as
Sequoiadendron giganteum. There's a price and species list at A to Z, and you can
walk around and look at species samples in the can there. The advantage to
buying from Hillside is that these are field-grown trees, and so never potbound. They're relatively inexpensive for their size, especially if you can
manage to fetch and carry them yourself. Or, if you prefer, Tree Movers will
deliver for you. Cozy.

CARMAN'S NURSERY
16201 Mozart Avenue
Los Gatos
(408) 356-0119
Tuesday–Saturday 9 A.M.–5 P.M. Sunday and Monday by appointment
Wheelchair accessible, with many tight spots to negotiate.

This is one of those out-at-the-elbows, out-of-the-way places that delight the plant addict with odd, new, specialized, and just plain weird things. And I don't mean the stuffed gazelle in the office. There are spooky plants like *Pseudopanax ferox*; there are sink gardens and planters; there are lots and lots of "liners"—tree seedlings in one- or two-inch pots, good for bonsai starts, or for their novelty alone, like some tiny purple-leafed birches I've seen there and coveted myself. There are grasses, vines, perennials, houseplants, and other plants, too; when I asked Mr. Carman what his specialty was, he said, gesturing at the muted riot of species around us, "Oh . . . odds and ends." As well as bonsai, he mentioned the use of his dwarf conifers and other dwarf trees in garden railroads: yes, the same sort of toy some of us had under the Christmas tree, translated to an outdoor landscape. Well, toot toot, I say. Not much is labeled, but the ever-attentive owner is easy to talk to, and clearly knows his stock. Not a place for tools and such, or big leafy background plants, but for some unassuming seedling that turns out to be something you've never seen before, this is the place.

SAKAMOTO PLANTS
15567 Camino Del Cerro
Los Gatos
(408) 356-3864
Thursday–Sunday 9 A.M.–5 P.M.
Wheelchair accessible, but narrow spaces that even a walker has to wriggle through.

An idiosyncratic place full of unexpected delights, disguised as a traditional Japanese nursery. There is a base of tradition, with a good stock of Japanese maples, junipers, and bonsai material; roses, perennials, shrubs, and vines; a fair selection of fruit trees including good citrus; rustic and refined containers, some very large and inviting; tools, chemicals, and soil amendments. The surprises lie in the array of tropicals and water-garden specialties, and in bits of imaginative planting and art. There's a bonsai'd tree labeled "orangequat," with foliage small even for a kumquat, and a nice dense branching habit. There's a screen, or maybe it's a flat mobile, made of bamboo and cobbles neatly hung on wires. Young and dwarfed trees are planted in handsome style- and color-coordinated containers: a bottlebrush in a pot glazed just the right red, a cascading juniper clasping the flat side of a tall, slate-blue pot as if it had been carved out in bas-relief. Grace notes like this delight the observant eye everywhere. You won't necessarily find this year's trendy cherub or gargoyle, or even many informative labels or tags; you will find attentive staff, originality, and a good eye.

ALMADEN VALLEY NURSERY
15800 Almaden Expressway
San Jose
(408) 997-1234
Monday–Friday 9 A.M.–5:30 P.M. Saturday 8 A.M.–6 P.M. Sunday 8 A.M.–5 P.M.
Wheelchair accessible

Largish and a little on the dressy side, this one has a few surprises among its healthy plants: Italian vegetable and British flower seeds, for example. The demo plantings at the front entrance are handsome and done with a thoughtful touch—the plant labels tell you where the species you're admiring can be found in the nursery. When you enter through the gift shop, you meet another surprise, a coffee counter (yes, cappuccino and such) that opens on weekday mornings at 7 A.M., and on weekends at 8 A.M. There's a table or two to sit at among the containers and knickknacks, and there are *Sunset* books, a house newsletter, and garden advice sheets—some of them very good—to read while you sip. Through the door you find mounds of well-displayed seasonal color, annual and perennial, the usual veggie starts (including tomatillos, though), and an herb selection on the high side of normal and priced very well. There's also a reasonable choice of fruit trees, shade trees, and flowering trees, with a few attention-getters like *Chitalpa tashkentensis*; and a similarly reasonable choice of perennials and roses. One strength is in water plants, and in prefab ponds, liners, and some handsomely naturalistic waterfall pumps, shown off in a couple of nice ponds. In keeping with the demo area at the entrance, the plants are well labeled, and there's good information posted all over. I've heard staffers give some sound and encouraging plant-use and design advice, too.

CACTUS FLAT NURSERY
1895 Crinan Drive
San Jose
(408) 287-2220
Call for appointment
Almost too tightly packed to walk through unless you want a few extra piercings; I wouldn't try to get a wheelchair through here.

Paul and Retha Long are more casually welcoming than a "call for appointment" business card might imply; they are, however, not always home, and this is a home-based enterprise. They have another growing ground elsewhere, but there's hardly room to turn around here for all the variously prickly and strange plants in pots and flats and seedling trays, up and down paths, in the ground, and in the greenhouse and propagation frame. It's amazing. It's comical. It's gorgeous. It'd be hell on a burglar at night. There are plants from Madagascar and South Africa and the Americas—there's a boojum!—and from Mars, you'd swear. The Longs know their charges well, and have stories about how to grow them, where they're from, and what they're good for, as if such wonderful weirdness needed to be good for anything. Succulents are all they sell. The talk, lore, and enthusiasm are gifts.

CAPITOL WHOLESALE NURSERY
3395 Keaton Loop
San Jose
(408) 238-7966
FAX (408) 532-1205
Monday–Friday 7:30 A.M.–6 P.M. Saturday 8 A.M.–6 P.M. Sunday 9 A.M.–5 P.M.
Wheelchair accessible

Prices really are good; the plant palette here is pretty much standard, but includes things like the giant honeysuckle of Burma (not really rare, but who could resist?), specimen trees like weeping cherry, and a fair array of perennials. You can get a quantity discount, and the staff here shows lots of patience with amateurs, always a virtue in a wholesale operation that invites the public. There are some annuals, quick color, and ground covers too, and soil amendments in sacks. The situation, a smallish paved lot on a creek bank with a cute little red house parked incongruously in the middle and crowded by canned plants, is more friendly and less dusty than some wholesalers, so it's easier to browse.

CENTRAL WHOLESALE NURSERY
1670 McKinley Avenue
San Jose
(408) 280-1131
Retail hours Saturday 7:30 A.M.–3 P.M.
Wheelchair accessible

Here's where to buy stock for the petunia farm of your dreams. I've seen nothing out of the ordinary here, and no edibles or fruit trees except for a few citrus, but the plants look healthy and the staff is kind enough to amateurs to have posted instructions for loading a nursery cart (which can be tricky). Tags are rudimentary to nonexistent: signs designate annuals, perennials, trees; that's about it. There are redwoods up to twenty-four-inch box size; Japanese maples, including some of the coral-bark and other fancy sorts; lots of junipers, oleanders, and similar sturdy shrubs; perennials, ferns and other shade-lovers, and bedding plants, at wholesale prices; also tree stakes and some soil amendments including bulk finished compost. I'd look here to fill lots of bare space in a hurry, get one or two specimens of redwood or maple, or plant a low-maintenance garden. Prices are not posted, but are in the sales computer; do some comparison shopping first, then ask.

MANTHEY'S NURSERY
327 San Jose Avenue
San Jose
(408) 293-6269
Monday–Saturday 8:30 A.M.–5 P.M. Sunday 8:30 A.M.–4 P.M.
Wheelchair accessible

A little out-of-the-way, as many worthwhile things are, this is a good general nursery and a great azalea nursery. Azaleas go on forever here, swarming around the other good-looking stock—some color, nice perennials—in gallon sizes and in standard training and general profusion. Manthey's breeds its azaleas, including the Southern Indicas that are more sun-tolerant than most, and its stock looks healthy and ambitious. There are some soil amendments and plant foods and such, but the reason to make a trip here is the azaleas. Staff—family—are smart and friendly; ask questions here for good information. And don't miss the feathered inhabitants of the shop, at least nine big psittacines: macaws and Amazons (who bite; beware), and one very affectionate cockatoo. When the azaleas and the birds are all in bloom, it's a good place to get drunk on color.

ORCHIDS FOR EVERYONE
1141 South De Anza Boulevard
San Jose
(408) 446-5866
FAX (408) 446-4412
Monday–Friday 10 A.M.–7 P.M. Saturday 10 A.M.–5 P.M. Sunday noon–5 P.M.
Wheelchair accessible

These aren't quite the hothouse dainties they appear to be; Orchids for Everyone specializes in "windowsill and outdoor orchids." The display is spectacular. Even individual plants are spectacular, with their flamboyant, elegant, or just outrageous blooms. Prices are *not* outrageous; nothing here is cheap, but there are bargains to be found among plants just out of bloom, or young ones; all the stock looks robustly healthy, and I wouldn't call anything overpriced for its size or species. The orchids are helpfully tagged as to their rarity, difficulty, demands, and care, and there is lots of information to be had from staff and from a browsing library that includes video discs and a player. An array of books is also for sale. There are containers and cachepots ranging from elaborate to artfully understated, and orchid-specialty fertilizers for your new pet. If it wants a pet of its own, there are a few appropriate houseplants—ferns for example—for company.

PAYLESS NURSERY/PAYLESS ACE HARDWARE AND ROCKERY

2927 South King Road
San Jose
(408) 274-7815
FAX (408) 223-1971
Monday–Friday 7 A.M.–7 P.M. Saturday and Sunday 7 A.M.–6 P.M.
Wheelchair accessible

One-stop shopping of a sort. Bulk soil amendments, gravel, rocks, pavers, concrete, and building materials; a standard hardware store with garden tools, barbecues, some furniture. Across the parking lot, there's a pretty good nursery. Most of the offerings here are the standard stuff, but there's a wide enough selection to keep it interesting. There are houseplants, ornaments, birdfeeders, fertilizers, and pesticides, including some less-toxic ones. Staff are attentive and seem fairly well informed.

POTTERY MART

3640 Stevens Creek Boulevard
San Jose
(408) 296-7144
Monday–Saturday 9 A.M.–6 P.M. Sunday 10 A.M.–5 P.M.
Wheelchair accessible

A cactus and a pot to put it in. Pottery Mart has lots of honest red clay pots in sizes from houseplant to hot tub, plus glazed and decorated containers, the sort of aggregate plant pots and wastecans you see on city streets, ornate fountains, and birdbaths. Aside from containers, there are a few kinds of pavers, including handsome chipped-slate rounds, and the life-size naturalistically painted Alsatian dog you've always wanted. If that's not what you've always wanted, maybe another of the assortment of statuary will do: frogs and fish and turtles and dragons and lions, a Saint Francis or Joseph or Theresa, a Kuan Yin, a Buddha, or the goddess Hebe plumbed for fountain use. Bonus points to Pottery Mart's cheerful and attentive staff for correct identification labels on all of these, and on the myriad cacti and succulents, some as striking and unusual as the towering variegated euphorbias greeting greenhouse visitors. If not quite on a level with wonderfully crazed places like Cactus Flat or Cactus Unlimited or the Dry Garden, Pottery Mart is still a must-see for succulent fanciers.

SUNSHINE NURSERY

2157 Alum Rock Avenue
San Jose
(408) 258-5896
Daily 8 A.M.–5 P.M.
Wheelchair accessible

This one looks like the place to go for interesting vegetable seedlings: on a single visit I saw upo, luffa, bitter melon, Japanese netted melon, soybeans, kabocha, longbeans, sesame, and peppers from Fushimi to chile de arbol, habañero, serrano, shishito, and Italian wax. There were at least a dozen kinds, some in gallon cans for the impatient or the late starter and as many kinds of tomatoes; there were greens and other veggies and herbs including red and green shiso; there were ranks of fruit trees, several breeds of English walnut, grapes, and strawberries. I had to go find lunch immediately. Information tags for the edibles are pretty good, and it's easy enough to get questions answered accurately by staffers. There are shade trees, too, lots of ornamentals (including a startling and stately ivy lollipop at least a yard across, standing unaided on its own trunk), grasses, shrubs, the works. Inside the shop are houseplants, including orchids and bonsai-like ficus; seeds, tools, and a modest selection of containers, fertilizers, and pesticides. The place is complete, but what it's best for is furnishing your self-sufficient urban survival food farm—in style.

FRANK DIFIORE'S SYMONS' NURSERY

806 West San Carlos
San Jose
(408) 295-1875
Monday–Saturday 8 A.M.–6 P.M. Sunday 9 A.M.–5 P.M.
The outdoor section is wheelchair accessible.

Ramble over the tracks and past the appliances' graveyard out on West San Carlos, and on a dusty lot you'll find Birnham Wood ready to hitch up its kilts and thumb a ride to Dunsinane. It's a portable instant forest, big trees in big boxes, the sort of thing a home gardener might need one or two of when faced with a bald lot and sagging morale. Some are distinguished mainly by their size, but there are unusual things like a mahonia—normally a shrub—trained up as an eight-foot tree with a two-inch-diameter trunk. There are fruit trees, some of interesting varieties and species; one doesn't often see several varieties of almond trees in a retail nursery. Name tags are pretty good, but information and (in the big-trees section) even price tags are scarce; if that's where you're heading, grab a staffer by the elbow. I have quibbles with some of the pruning on a few of the big trees here; if you choose one, look carefully for stubs, breaks, and scars.

Aside from trees, diFiore's Symons' carries lots of shrubs, including handsome cycads; shade plants like big ferns; perennials and bedding plants; a modest assortment of edibles including artichokes; and some good midrange tools, containers, and ornaments. There is a table with chairs and a heap of garden books inside the shop, set up and clearly well-used for reference and planning. The atmosphere of the place is more funky than fashionable, one of very few places where you can buy both a decent German iris and a card with a joke about relatives, work, or perverse luck—the sort you find on the wall in certain bars.

NAME-DROPPING

In the text of nursery reviews, there are a few brand names I cite as good things in themselves and as an implicit recommendation for the places that sell them. Annie's Annuals is one, a local small grower that specializes in plants beyond the usual run of impatiens and marigolds, and includes some California natives and their cultivars just because they're pretty. Look for big tags illustrated by enticing photographs and a paragraph or two of description—which is also an advantage. I sometimes mention that a nursery sells Botanical Interests or Shepherd's Garden Seeds, too. Both propagate unusual varieties of flowers and edibles; Botanical Interests raises theirs organically. Another seed company I mention is Kitazama, which sells "Asian" vegetables like loofa squash, asparagus beans, Chinese mustard greens, and nappa cabbage. Seeds of Change is a company that propagates heirloom, open-pollinated, and just plain interesting plants. Larner Seeds is a local concern with local concerns, specializing in California native wildflowers and even native trees.

YAMANAKA'S BONSAI NURSERY

966 South De Anza Boulevard
San Jose
(408) 252-1458
Friday–Wednesday 9 A.M.–5 P.M. Closed Thursday
Wheelchair accessible

It's a funny contrast: skyscraping dracaenas and palms indoors, and small but mighty bonsai pines outdoors. Among this good-sized nursery's stock of perennials, annuals, grasses, bamboos, shrubs, and trees are some painstakingly trained landscape pines, small bonsai starts, very refined prebonsai in gallon cans, and finished bonsai, some pretty impressive. There are mall bonsai, too, and some interesting and well-done turns like a bonsai'd Australian tea tree. Inside are bonsai pots, wires, soil mixes, and tools, ikebana vases, a long run of *Bonsai Today* magazine, and enough wind chimes to make your head ring in harmony. Yamanaka's nonbonsai stock is varied and healthy, too; you won't be surprised to find a lot of Japanese and related maples, but there are variegated jade plants and other attention-getters among the perennials, a decent choice of fruit trees including some rather large persimmons, and other basics. There are a few smallish ornaments, which is fitting; you wouldn't want to distract attention from the sort of plant you'll find here. Some tools and soil amendments too, and friendly, knowledgeable service of the proprietary sort.

EL REAL NURSERY

2611 El Camino Real
Santa Clara
(408) 243-4910
Monday–Saturday 8:30 A.M.–5:30 P.M. Sunday 9 A.M.–5 P.M.
Wheelchair accessible; some tight spots in interior.

A smallish nursery, visibly welcoming and nicely laid out. A set of intersecting paths frames the stock and allows spaces to display the plants' and merchandise's uses. Little triangle gardens are planted in the corners, wooden benches and arbors face the approaches. The rows of boxed shade trees and dwarf fruit trees segue nicely into the surrounding green: a stately Italian stone pine in back and wild box elders along the banks of Saratoga Creek, which flows alongside the nursery. One event to watch for is El Real's annual sale of tropical plants—hibiscus, bougainvilleas, and the like—in August. Informational tagging is spotty, but includes things like very good advice about live Christmas trees; staffers are friendly and seem to know their stuff, so ask. Near the entrance are slightly pricey but well-matched and handsome combinations of succulents in planter bowls; in the greenhouse, some interesting houseplants, more succulents. Outdoors, you'll find tree ferns and other shade-lovers, a reasonable selection of perennials, annuals, shrubs, standard veggies, and herbs at very good prices; also, a small quantity of red-clay, plastic, and some handsome glazed pots, hand tools, and soil amendments and such. If you listen in the right season, you can hear frogs singing in the creek.

SUNNYVALE NURSERY

1485 Saratoga-Sunnyvale Road
Sunnyvale
(408) 245-1689
Monday–Saturday 9 A.M.–5:30 P.M. Sunday 9 A.M.–5 P.M.
Wheelchair accessible

Once you finish blinking at the interestingly pruned olive trees growing on the lot, look around for lots of pond plants and equipment, a good range of shade trees, perennials, color, and edibles, the last including some unusual varieties at very good prices. Say hello to the resident koi and goldfish in the demonstration pond (and say good-bye, too; they're not for sale, though staff will direct you to retail sources if you want some). Walk around to the herbs and scented geraniums, shrubs, roses, vines, and other regular inhabitants of a large nursery; you'll see houseplants, too, not cheap but healthy and inspiring, and some quite sizable. Staffers pay attention without being intrusive, and seem to know their materials. Nonplant offerings include fountains, a variety of trellises and *tuteurs* of wood and iron, prefab pergolas, birdfeeders and birdhouses, tools including not only Felco pruning shears but replacement parts for them, ornaments, books, fertilizers, supplements, and pesticides.

TOOLS, SUPPLIES, AND DECOR

BAY AREA IN GENERAL

MAISON D'ETRE
92 South Park
San Francisco
(415) 357-1747
Monday–Saturday noon–6 P.M. Closed Sunday
Wheelchair accessible, but cluttered inside

5330 College Avenue
Oakland
(510) 658-0698
Wednesday–Saturday noon–6 P.M. Closed Sunday–Tuesday
Not wheelchair accessible

Along with stationery, scents, and indoor antiques and decor, these two stores (as their name would suggest) stock some garden ornaments and occasionally a piece or two of outdoor furniture. The aesthetic is of the delicate wire and drifty gauze sort, nice with a pale terra-cotta pot of lavender on a sheltered verandah.

URBAN FARMER STORE

2833 Vicente
San Francisco
(415) 661-2204
Monday–Friday 7:30 A.M.–6 P.M. Saturday 9:30 A.M.–5 P.M. Closed Sunday

653 East Blithedale Avenue
Mill Valley
(415) 380-3840
FAX (415) 380-3848
Monday–Friday 7:30 A.M.–6 P.M. Saturday 8 A.M.–5 P.M. Sunday 9 A.M.–5 P.M.

A Tinkertoy wonderland of irrigation parts and supplies: PVC piping, joints, emitters, and widgets, and the tools to put them all together. Also pond and fountain equipment, electronic dog fences, low-watt outdoor lighting, hand tools, reel mowers, and useful substances like Cloud Cover antiwilt spray, and copper tape and diatomaceous earth for snail barriers.

WILD BIRD CENTER

Locations throughout the Bay Area; see below.
All open Monday-Saturday 10 A.M. - 6 P.M. Sunday noon-5 P.M.
Wheelchair accessible

This is one part of a national chain, and a very good idea in franchise stores; the central office encourages community involvement. Staff includes some enthusiastic birders, who conduct classes and birdwalks. In the store, you can find bird feeders, birdhouses, birdbath, and water drippers to make thim more inviting. There are also books, CDs, field glasses, accessories form wind chimes to sweatshirts, and seed and other bird food.

---

926 El Camino Real
San Carlos
(650) 595-0300

798 Blossom Hill Road
King's Court Center
Los Gatos
(408) 358-9453

1270A Newell Avenue
San Miguel Shopping Center
Walnut Creek
(510) 937-7333

WILD BIRDS UNLIMITED
Locations throughout the Bay Area; see below.
Monday-Friday 9:30 A.M.–6 P.M. Saturday 9:30 A.M.–5 P.M.
Sunday Noon–5 P.M.
Store is wheelchair accessible, but classes are held upstairs.

Birding enthusiasts have been recruited to run and staff these stores, and there are ties to the local Audubon Society. This policy taps some of the local wealth of expertise about birds, and spreads it around via monthly guided walks t area parks and other birding hotspots. More concretely, they also sell birdseed and feeders, birdbaths, bird houses and other nesting aids, field guides and binoculars. You might not want pigeons in you r grass or a great blue heron in your koi pond, but every garden needs birds.

---

692 Contra Costa Boulevard,
Pleasant Hill (510) 798-0303

20672 Homestead Road, Cupertino
(408) 252-5712

71 Brookwood Avenue,
Santa Rosa (707) 576-0681

7182 Regional Street, Dublin
(510) 803-6901

SAN FRANCISCO

CONNECTICUT STREET PLANT SUPPLIES
306 Connecticut Street
San Francisco
(415) 821-4773
Tuesday–Saturday 9 A.M.–6 P.M. Sunday 9 A.M.–4:30 P.M.

Everything for plants—except plants. Analogous to one of those pet-supply stores that sell you bones but not Bowsers, this little shop, fronted by Bell and Trunk Flowers, stocks plant food, soil amendments, potting soil, compost bins, cures including environmentally friendly Safer pesticides, and hand tools. Think of it as a grocery store for your garden.

LUMBINI

156 South Park
San Francisco
(415) 896-2666
Monday–Friday 9 A.M.–6:30 P.M. Saturday 11 A.M.–6:30 P.M.; may close earlier
on a slow day
Wheelchair accessible, but tight.

Landscape magician Topher Delany calls this a shop for the inner gardener
in everyone. This strikes some literalists as uncomfortably close to being a
store for intestinal flora, but I like to visit the place all the same. It's far
from being exclusively a garden store, but among the various whimsical
and startling objects to be had are seeds from Asia (including some of those
hard-to-find Vietnamese herbs), Australia, and elsewhere—quite an assortment and all of brands you don't find often. There's also a wide and
imaginative range of garden books, from amusing to dead-on practical. You
can find ornaments—concrete bunnies, gazing balls, prayer flags, chairs,
and stylish containers. Some proceeds go to fund worthy garden projects,
like the African Healing Garden at Highland Hospital in Oakland.

SOKO HARDWARE

1698 Post Street at Buchanan
(415) 931-5510
San Francisco
Monday–Saturday 9 A.M.–5:30 P.M. Closed Sunday
Upstairs is wheelchair accessible.

This hardware store whose stock includes dentists' picks and hemostats and
funny jingly keychains also has a few handy things for the gardener: containers, including seriously big pots; bamboo deer scares; ornaments; and some
clever hand tools, sickles, and cultivators; fertilizers; supplements; and
Kitazama brand vegetable seeds. There are rain chains, stone basins and
lanterns, and hibachi and standard American barbecue equipment. I can
never thread my way through the downstairs jumble to the hose fittings
and long-handled hedge shears without being sidetracked for at least
twenty minutes in the kitchen equipment, and that's fun too.

EAST BAY

L. H. VOSS MATERIALS, INC. LANDSCAPE CENTERS
Locations throughout the East Bay; see below.

Not, in spite of that Nav-Land name, a part of the Navlet's empire (Voss leases some of its spaces from Navlet's, in a business alliance of long standing), all these locations sell soil, amendments, compost, sand, mulch, sod, gravels, paving and pavers, bricks, railroad ties, and those clever interlocking blocks for retaining walls. They also sell rocks—I've seen sandstones, slates, flashy cherts, and obsidian, among others. Stock isn't identical in all locations; if you're looking for inspiration, or something very specific, try more than one. The Mountaire location in Concord also has a small nursery with trees, citrus, roses, perennials, ground covers, and some mildly unusual plants like artichokes. The nursery is paved with a series of demonstration plots, so you can get a sense of how some of their materials will look and feel underfoot.

All stores open Monday–Saturday 8 A.M.–5 P.M.; Sunday 9 A.M.–4:30 P.M. Rockyards are mostly wheelchair accessible; some offices may not be, as they're trailers.

Nav-Land Landscape Center
2445 Vista Del Monte, Concord
(510) 687-2930

Mountaire Garden Supply
4749 Clayton Road, Concord
(510) 682-5552

Nav-Land Landscape Center
800 Camino Ramon, Danville
(510) 820-8955

Nav-Land Landscape Center
46408 Warm Springs Boulevard,
Fremont (510) 490-0310

L. H. Voss Materials, Inc.
5511 Sunol Boulevard, Pleasanton
(510) 846-1414

Nav-Land Landscape Center
2665 Pittsburg-Antioch Highway,
Antioch (510) 778-3123

Brentwood Decorative Rock
Highway 4, Brentwood
(510) 634-0131

GOLDEN GATE LAWNMOWER
544D Cleveland Avenue
Albany
(510) 525-0487
Tuesday–Saturday 9 A.M.–5 P.M.

Get that nice quiet push mower's blades sharpened up right and you'll never bother with the Thing That Goes Vroom again. Plus, you can mow the lawn early on a weekend morning when you'd rather be in bed. This place works on power mowers, too.

A NEW LEAF GALLERY
1286 Gilman Street
Berkeley
(510) 525-7621
Wednesday–Saturday 10 A.M.–6 P.M. Sunday 11 A.M.–5 P.M.
Closed Monday and Tuesday
Partly wheelchair accessible; the flag-and-gravel path includes stepping stones over "creek."

Something for every taste in original garden art. With lots of moving water in its various fountains for sale and underfoot in the artificial creeklet, the display area is relaxing and usually amusing to wander through; the sculpture seems always to include something humorous. Some of it is also functional furniture. There are small pieces on display near the office, for the limited garden space or budget.

AMERICAN SOIL PRODUCTS, INC.
2222 Third Street
Berkeley
(510) 883-7200
Monday–Saturday 7:30 A.M.–5 P.M. Sunday 9 A.M.–5 P.M.
The rockyard is wheelchair negotiable, if lumpy and crowded sometimes. The office, where the cash register and some samples are, is not.

Here's where to go when you need a Serious Rock. American Soil's always-changing stock of boulders, flagstones, cobbles, and just plain head-size rocks is almost gaudy in its variety. Green and red and spangled with mica, some of this stuff must be extraplanetary. Stacked or tilted right, these stones become furniture, planters, pondlets, and birdbaths. There's also some stone sculpture—table-and-chair, lanterns, pediments.

American Soil, of course, sells soil too, in truckloads (take-out or delivered for a fee) or in easier-to-manage bags. If you need just a cubic yard or two, you'll save significantly by picking it up as a truckload yourself. A cubic yard will fit in most pickup beds; make sure your suspension is up to having it dumped in from a front-loader. The variety of soil mixes, amendments, mulches, and gravels is as extensive as the variety of rocks, and the yard is heady with fragrances that will make a gardener smile. Staffers are informed and patient with amateurs. You'll find other useful things like bricks, landscape fabrics, and half-barrels here, too.

ANIMAL FARM'S WILD BIRD ANNEX
1527 San Pablo Avenue
Berkeley
(510) 528-3300
Monday–Friday 10 A.M.–6:30 P.M. Saturday 9:30 A.M.–6 P.M. Sunday 11 A.M.–5 P.M.
Wheelchair accessible

This small space, a recent spinoff from a pet-supplies store, is packed with seed, suet, and nectar feeders, as well as squirrel repellents and baffles. The annex also sells nest boxes and a limited range of field guides. In addition to the bird-related products, bat and butterfly houses are available.

AW POTTERY
2908 Adeline Street
Berkeley
(510) 549-3901
FAX (510) 549-6877
Monday–Saturday 8 A.M.–5 P.M. Sunday noon–3 P.M.
Wheelchair accessible, but space is very tight; some corners are claustrophobic even if you're on foot.

601 50th Avenue
Oakland
(510) 533-3900
FAX (510) 533-8190
Monday–Saturday 8 A.M.–5 P.M. Closed Sunday
Wheelchair accessible

Pots, pots, lots of pots. The prices aren't appreciably cheaper here than at the retail stores that carry Aw's pots, imported from Asia, but there's a huge selection for those determined enough to wedge between the towers and ranks of merchandise. You'll have to look carefully for price tags, and inspect for chips and (where it's wanted) watertightness, but a lot of what's here exhibits a rustic look that works well in many gardens, and indoors too. If you need a great big brown urn, or a portable pottery pond, here's a good place to look.

BERKELEY INDOOR GARDEN CENTER

844 University Avenue
Berkeley
(510) 549-2918
Outside CA (800) 523-1367
FAX (510) 540-8409
Monday–Friday 10 A.M.–6 P.M. Saturday 10 A.M.–5 P.M. Closed Sunday
Partly wheelchair accessible; there's an interior step at the back.

These folks seem pretty down-to-earth as hydroponics partisans go, selling inexpensive components, less-toxic pesticides, and organic fertilizers and supplements, helping with assembly and ideas, and explicitly recommending their methods as a supplement to dirt gardening. The staffers I talked to mentioned early seed-starting, orchid culture, chili peppers and other heat-loving and sun-demanding goodies, and speculated about the legality of growing tobacco—the ultimate roll-your-own. They do catalog sales, and promise that they will service any brand of system, not just their own. Besides gadgets and tinkertoys, buckets, lights, pumps, heat mats, reflectors, rockwool, rooting compounds, reservoirs, and whatnots, you can find Seeds of Change seeds, two kinds of bat guano, and interested people with bright ideas.

CLAY OF THE LAND

2619 Seventh Street
Berkeley
(510) 843-2699
Monday–Saturday 10 A.M.–5 P.M. Sunday noon–5 P.M.
Wheelchair accessible, but bumpy and narrow.

Pots for plants and for water gardens—many sizes, handsome designs, reasonable prices. Also fountains and other pottery stuff—plaques, ornaments, and such. This little sliver of a lot on Seventh Street, not far from Magic Gardens, Dwight Way Nursery, Saffron Cafe, and the Ecology Center, is full of pleasant surprises.

DIAMOND BERKELEY

1827 Fifth Street, Unit B
Berkeley
(510) 704-0117
Tuesday–Friday 11 A.M.–5 P.M. Saturday and Monday 11 A.M.–3 P.M.
Closed Sunday

Why the odd hours? "So I can go sailing," says the manager, and it does seem to be that sort of casual store. There's much less display space than in most hydroponics stores, but you can see rooting compound, supplements, fertilizers, some components, and less-toxic pesticides here. The afternoon sailor also said his mind was Diamond's chief asset, and I have seen him doing some detailed consulting with a contractor. The out-of-the-way location has one major advantage: it's next-door to the East Bay Vivarium. I wonder if one can rent a snake to clean out one's hydrotubing? Please don't tell the Vivarium folks I said to ask.

ECOLOGY CENTER

Ecology Center Bookstore
2530 San Pablo Avenue
Berkeley
(510) 548-3402

Tuesday–Saturday 11 A.M.–6 P.M.
Wheelchair accessible

Ecology Center Farmers' Markets
(510) 546-3333
TUESDAYS (Derby Street at Martin Luther King Jr. Way)
1 P.M.–dusk in winter; 2 P.M.–7 P.M. in summer (the hours change with Daylight
Savings Time)
THURSDAYS (Fourth Street and University Avenue)
2 P.M.–7 P.M. in summer
SATURDAYS (Martin Luther King Jr. Way at Center Street)
10 A.M.–2 P.M.
Wheelchair accessible

Ecology Center Information, *Terrain* Magazine
(510) 548-2220

Ever wonder where the sixties went to compost? The Ecology Center runs three farmers' markets on the streets of Berkeley (which are good enough for the likes of Alice Waters) plus a number of other operations, including the magazine *Terrain* (for which I write a garden column) and a smallish bookstore at its program center on San Pablo Avenue. You can find garden books ranging from indispensable to obscure, gadgets, fertilizers, and heirloom seeds. But the best thing here, aside from encouragement, is information. There's an established library and info center, and if you come in with a garden question and just ask out loud, there's a good chance someone in one department or another will have an answer; the place is riddled with gardeners. There are good cheap classes here, too, on Saturdays in spring and summer, taught by authors like Judith Goldsmith (*Strawberries in November*), experts from UC, and hands-in-the-dirt gardeners with bright ideas.

At the farmers' markets you can find herb, veggie, and flower starts, including exotics like Thai basil. Spiral Gardens sells inexpensive and interesting gallon-size plants and gives out good advice free; several other small growers, like Berkeley's Flatland Flower Farm, sell whatever they like best— old roses, herbs, irises, Kitty Grass—and a master gardener from UC's ag extension is often on hand on Tuesdays. Berkeley Youth Alternative's Youth

Project Garden sells plants as well as produce. You'll find more plants in spring and summer; they're locally grown and therefore seasonal. There are always odd and heirloom vegetables and fruits for sale at the markets, with seeds worth saving if you're that ambitious.

GARDEN HOME
1799D Fourth Street
Berkeley
(510) 559-7050
Sunday–Friday 10 A.M.–6 P.M. Saturday 9 A.M.–6 P.M.
Wheelchair accessible

With the small urban garden, deck, or terrace in mind, Garden Home pulls indoors and outdoors together with furniture and some plants that would be at home in either. Emphasis is on decor, rather than food or preservation gardening, but a practical bent comes through in the array of hand tools, materials, and containers. Prices range from rather high to quite reasonable, including for plant materials. It's also a good place to buy some lavender lotion and soap for after gardening. Demonstrations and short classes on weekends and some weekdays, many of them more about natural decor than dirt; call or ask for a schedule.

THE GARDENER
1836 Fourth Street
Berkeley
(510) 548-4545
Monday–Saturday 10 A.M.–6 P.M. Thursday 10 A.M.–7 P.M. Sunday 11 A.M.–6 P.M.
Wheelchair accessible

There is a remnant population of actual garden things here, among the scents and the perfect furniture. What there is is pretty well-selected: topnotch tools, Shepherd's Garden Seeds, outdoor furniture, and ornaments. Walk in for a trowel; walk out with a Zen bamboo pitcher, a $6 bar of soap, and plans to redo your house to accommodate that slate-topped table.

HIDA BONSAI GARDEN TOOL COMPANY

1333 San Pablo Avenue
Berkeley
(510) 524-3700
Monday–Saturday 9 A.M.–5 P.M. Closed Sunday
Wheelchair accessible, but it's a very small store with narrow aisles—and lots of sharp objects.

There's a small, interesting selection of garden tools in what started exclusively as a woodworking-tools shop, then branched into bonsai equipment. Things you never knew you needed—that great Japanese weeding knife, sturdy enough to step on for leverage, small enough for tight corners; long-reach precision pruners; an assortment of Japanese pruning saws; one-hand hoes; sickles; and sharp weeders. Tool sharpening, including pruning saws. A family business with good information and a personal touch.

OHMEGA SALVAGE

2400 San Pablo Avenue
Berkeley
(510) 843-7368

OHMEGA TOO

2204 San Pablo Avenue
Berkeley
(510) 843-3636
FAX for both: (510) 843-0666
Monday–Saturday 9 A.M.–5 P.M. Sunday noon–5 P.M.
Wheelchair accessible

Some things at Ohmega are reliable; you can count on finding bricks, tiles, the odd gate or bit of fence. Some things are completely unpredictable: a cast-iron reclining titan, a baptismal font for that outrageous birdbath. That's the nature of salvage.

Ohmega Too, just down the street, deals in both salvaged and new-reproduction stuff; to see the garden ornaments, fountains, birdbaths, pools, containers, and trellises, tear yourself away from that Rube Goldberg Victorian shower and go through to the garden behind the building. Outdoor lighting and gate and hose bibb hardware are inside. It's a great place to be distracted.

OUR OWN STUFF GARDEN GALLERY
3017 Wheeler Street
Berkeley
(510) 540-8544
Open Sunday afternoons
It would be extremely difficult to fit a wheelchair into this private backyard, and there are a few steps.

Here's a gem worth visiting even if you're not about to buy. It's difficult to come up with the right superlative for this pocket-sized garden full of Marcia Donahue's and Mark Bulwinkle's sculpture and an impressive collection of weird and whimsical plants. You can get a taste of it in *Gardening from the Heart: Why Gardeners Garden* (see the Gardener's Bookshelf chapter) but it has changed some since that book was published—it's changed some since this paragraph was written, no doubt. I see something new every time I venture in.

URBAN ORE
Sixth and Gilman Streets
Berkeley
Building Materials Exchange, (510) 559-4460
General Store, (510) 559-4450
Salvage and Recycling, (510) 559-4451
Daily 8:30 A.M.–5 P.M.
Wheelchair accessible; some rough and tight spaces.

This is the first place to go when you really need a whatchamacallit. It's a reliable place for salvage classics like old bricks and flue tiles, usually with a big selection of these and other building bits—doors, sinks, steps, and the hardware for them—along with objects of gardening value like gates, fencing material, and sound, used lumber of all sorts. For the garden or for any other part of your life, you never know what you'll find here; my best prize so far is a brilliant hand-woven coat that I believe to be Afghani, in mint condition, for under $10. Look for containers and other sundries, too.

GN BUTTERFLY FARM
P. O. Box 604
Danville, CA 94526-0604
(510) 820-4307
Wednesday–Saturday 11 A.M.–6 P.M.
bgendron@pacbell.net

A logical intersection of the ideas of garden ornaments and ladybugs-for-sale, this is a place you can order butterflies—monarchs, pipevine swallowtails, anise swallowtails, and Gulf fritillaries, as eggs, larvae, pupae, or adults, from March through October. You can also get several species of milkweed, the monarch caterpillar's host, and pipevine, an odd California native and host to the pipevine swallowtail. (Anise swallowtails like fennel, wild or tame; Gulf fritillaries like passion vine, and have followed its cultivation here from the South.)

LARM'S BUILDING AND GARDEN SUPPLY
743 High Street
Oakland
(510) 532-7474
FAX (510) 532-5567
Tuesday–Saturday 8 A.M.–5 P.M. Sunday 9 A.M.–3 P.M. Closed Mondays
Wheelchair accessible, though you may not need to get out of the car.

The attention-getter at this small yard just off I-880 is the even smaller demonstration patio just above eye level in front; it's the only bit of green in sight. What you can buy here are the materials and equipment to build your own patio, retaining wall, terrace, paved path, or fallout shelter. No soil amendments, but one good-looking type of topsoil; plus gravel, sand, cement, pavers, flagstones, bricks (some handsome and unusual high-fired-looking ones among the choices), blocks, those clever mortarless retaining-wall erector sets, and tools like shovels, floats, trowels and picks to put it all together.

ROCKROSE

5332 College Avenue
Oakland
(510) 595-8755
Wednesday–Saturday 11 A.M.–6 P.M.
Wheelchair accessible

This Rockridge store is inspiring and relaxing to visit, and clearly the work of a passionate gardener. You'll find containers, ornaments—tiles, sculptures, and plant tags—small fountains, and very well chosen birdfeeders. This is the sort of place that can put you in a garden mood even on a rainy day.

DAVIS STREET SMART RECYCLING CENTER

2615 Davis Street
San Leandro
(510) 638-2303
Daily 8 A.M.–5 P.M.
You can stay in your car, so wheelchair access is more or less moot.

You can dump yard waste here, or buy soil products, mulches, and composts by the bag or by the yard; delivery is available, too. To use the place, drive up to the scale house and ask for directions.

MORGAN'S MASONRY SUPPLY

2233 San Ramon Valley Boulevard
San Ramon
(510) 837-7296
Monday–Friday 7 A.M.–5 P.M. Saturday 9 A.M.–noon Closed Sunday
The yard is wheelchair accessible; the shop has several steep steps up.

All sorts of rocks, from boulders to flagstones to rocks for walls to cobbles to gravel. There are swatches of rock and brick and block and pavers all over the place, starting with the front wall, a patchwork of labeled samples that creates rather a startling (if useful) effect.

WILD WILD BIRDS

530 San Anselmo Avenue
San Anselmo
(415) 721-2473
Monday–Friday 11 A.M.–5:30 P.M. Saturday 10 A.M.–5 P.M.
Sunday 11:30 A.M.–5 P.M.

This may be the Bay Area's closest approach to a full-service birdfeeder store. The long narrow space holds a wide range of feeders, from the classic Droll Yankee cylinders to handcrafted, red cedar, Northwest Coast—style jobs. There is also bird-related art, a decent assortment of field guides, and a ledger where birders can record their sightings.

HYDROFARM GARDENING PRODUCTS

1455 East Francisco Boulevard
San Rafael
(415) 459-6095
(800) 634-9999
FAX (415) 459-6096
Hydrofarm@ aol.com
Monday–Friday 10 A.M.–6 P.M. Saturday 10 A.M.–3 P.M. Closed Sunday

Hydrofarm manufactures a lot of the light systems that other stores sell. You can get planter boxes, planting media, fertilizers, circulation systems, lights, and racks straight from the source here.

JACKSON'S HARDWARE

435 DuBois Street
San Rafael
(415) 454-3740
Monday–Friday 6 A.M.–6 P.M. Saturday 8 A.M.–5 P.M. Closed Sunday

Lots of serious tools and supplies here; the early opening hour says this place is geared toward contractors. There are good garden tools, some slightly hard-to-find, like corn knives, cane knives, and machetes. But the notable find is real tree tools: climbing gear, hard hats, chaps, anchors, long-reach pruners, saws, polesaws, thimbles and cabling equipment, chainsaws, and T-shirts with Oak Man/Euc Man jokes on them. If you don't understand those, you aren't ready for the chainsaw.

PENINSULA

GARDEN EQUIPMENT CLINIC
121 First Street
Los Altos
(650) 948-7950
Monday–Friday 8 A.M.–5 P.M. Saturday 8 A.M.–noon
Wheelchair accessible

This busy little shop in downtown Los Altos sells power mowers, tillers, blowers, shredders, Billy Goats, pole pruners, shears, hand tools, loppers, shovels, rakes, orchard ladders, and other handy items like trenching spades and long-reach pruners. It really is a clinic, too, for lawn mower and other small-engine repair and maintenance, mower-blade sharpening, and power-saw (not hand-saw) sharpening. To keep you out of the people clinic, Garden Equipment Clinic sells glasses, gloves, and other safety equipment, too.

CIARDELLA'S GARDEN SUPPLY
2027 East Bayshore Road
Palo Alto
(650) 321-5913
FAX (650) 321-0711
Monday–Saturday 8 A.M.–5 P.M.
Wheelchair accessible

There is a token nursery here, in case you can't bear to take your load of dirt home without a green garnish, but in the main what to look for is down-to-earth materials: rock, from fines to boulders; flagstones, stepstones, cobbles, and pavers; wall blocks, five kinds of sand; soil mixes and soil conditioners like humus and compost; cement, peat moss, gravel, bark chips, weed block; tools, rebar, planters, decor, water-garden stuff including plants; grass seed mixes and fertilizers. There's a little shop with Week's Seeds (that's the North Carolina outfit that sponsors giant-vegetable contests; info is posted), and some antique implements on display—have a look and guess what they're for. You can pick up, your bulk goods yourself, for that total garden experience, or they'll deliver; in fact, they'll deliver COD.

STREAM OF CONSCIOUSNESS

It's a foggy September morning, the sort of gray-lidded day that makes the world seem like a stuffy room. Scrub jays and bushtits are the only creatures optimistic enough to make noise. I'm wading through waist-high grass in a small backyard closed in by a house, a queue of anonymous trees, and a great wave of blackberry and honeysuckle. The yard's owner pulls a wad of watercress from a muddy concrete sill, and, in that moment, the space I'm standing in opens and connects to the rest of the world as a tiny, gathering stream clears, whorls, and spills into the pool below it. Live water turns the yard into Place.

The place has a name, *K:yana Itewana*, "Middle Spring," given by a Zuni friend of Claire Greensfelder, who lives here. Claire is a little apologetic about the grass obscuring her plantings; it's risen, crested, and set seed while she had her back turned for a few weeks' travel to a women's conference. It may be that a woman's work is never done, but a gardener's work, if dropped for a month, will do itself—in directions the gardener doesn't expect. Look at this place, though: it's green after an August on its own. My yard wouldn't do that.

This yard has three springs to drink; the house's builder had put all three rivulets into underground pipes. Claire tells about the change: "My friend Richard [Register], the eco-builder, came over with a few dozen of his friends and dug up the underground spring that seeps all around the hillside at the north end of my backyard. The idea was to create a waterfall and pond system. It turned out more like a mud puddle with a big leak, but the birds and dragonflies love it."

The central spring runs over a concrete curb left from a previous regime and now integrated into the ground by a coat of silt; it's here that the watercress had slowed the stream into silence before Claire weeded. Now it chimes into a little pool where it's joined by the other two streams, each running a channel only a few inches wide. The pool narrows, spills over another, longer drop into a smaller pool, and disappears into a pipe that conducts it into the street gutter.

What impresses immediately is how little water it takes to effect such a climate change. These flows look like a teaspoon a minute, but given a catchbasin and room to channel, they connect and attract and nourish quite a bit of life.

Water in motion is a beacon to many species, and it's not hard to arrange for it, given some knowledge of the water table and the smallest elevation change. How many of us live along the streamcourses shown on old local maps? They're down there somewhere, maybe somewhere within spade's reach. Tempting, given the results here.

Out on the street, Claire's creek emerges from an unpromising bit of pipe under the curb, as if it were the dregs of someone's lawn-watering. Knowing the real source of this little sluice makes it look quite different from the water I'd seen on my way in, when I'd wondered who was washing a car. It has worn a miniature canyon, two inches deep, between the macadam and the concrete curb. Along with the crabgrass and popweed in the crevices, watercress is thriving. There's still not a lot of water (it *is* September), but the steep slope lends the streamlet a lively pace. Within half a block, now that I'm looking, I spot two more water sources feeding it, the water springing directly from the unpromising pavement as if from Moses' rock. My feet itch and the ground begins to feel less solid, almost effervescent. What else is hidden here? What am I standing on? Something alive and moving and going its own independent way, indifferent to our attention, merry and preoccupied.

Live water.

SOUTH BAY

SOUTHERN LUMBER COMPANY
1402 South First Street
San Jose
(408) 294-1487
FAX (408) 283-8795
Monday–Friday 8 A.M.–6 P.M. Saturday 8 A.M.–5 P.M. Sunday 9 A.M.–5 P.M.

Lumber, of course; this is one of the most fragrant places in the area if, like me, you find everything about wood sensual. You'll also find woodworking (but not garden) tools, and joist hangers and such hardware; prefab pergolas and arbors in at least five styles, gate kits, unseasoned burls for bonsai stands; swings and play structures for the kids; ready-made doghouses and handsome wooden sheds, which they'll deliver—free, if you're close enough. House numbers and mailboxes, too.

GARDENER'S BOOKSHELF

In November, when the fall veggies and new natives are sitting in the garden blinking and looking startled, and the daylight's getting wan and scarce, and the seed catalogs are piling up, it's a good time to perform the ancient gardeners' ceremony of the Elevation of the Feet and pick up some garden books. The lush, peak-season fantasies that spread invitingly across the page look more cheerful than the yard is likely to for a few months, and the best-written ones remind us why we got into this muddy mess in the first place. Here are some of my own staples, starting with the most general.

SUNSET WESTERN GARDEN BOOK
editors of Sunset Books and *Sunset* Magazine, Lane Publishing Company

Of course everybody needs the *Sunset* bible. It has good lists and sorts out plants' common names well enough to be intelligible to everyone. It's also available in most libraries, so you don't even need to buy it. One useful thing the *Sunset* people have done is divide their turf into microclimate zones that almost describe actual conditions in many local gardens. We need this sort of treatment in an area where a plant that needs full sun in my yard might need part shade in yours, twenty miles away. The grain of salt you need with a *Sunset* book is your own garden, and your neighbors'. Look around: is your block full of sunburnt camellias? Does someone down the street have a banana growing by the door? Has anyone around you ever grown a good eggplant? Even in the foggy depths of the bayside, there are "banana belts" that are reliably warmer than the next part of town. Or maybe you're in the redwoods where nothing else grows but moss. Here's where your friendly local garden mavens come in. Ask and look.

STRAWBERRIES IN NOVEMBER
Judith Goldsmith, Heyday Books

GOLDEN GATE GARDENING
Pam Peirce, agAccess Books

A pair of books I use in tandem. Goldsmith's book is focused on the East Bay; Peirce's is more coastal. Both include plant and planting advice, recipes, all sorts of good and entertaining information. They're closer to essential here even than a subscription to *Horticulture*. The only thing they lack is pornography—gorgeous garden photographs. (Garden porn is what hortisexuals read, of course.)

THE COMPLETE GUIDE TO LANDSCAPE DESIGN, RENOVATION, AND MAINTENANCE: A PRACTICAL HANDBOOK FOR THE HOME LANDSCAPE GARDENER
Cass Turnbull, Betterway Publications

Sound principles and bright ideas clearly explained: this is one of those little-known masterpieces. Turnbull founded PlantAmnesty (see page 70) and is a professional gardener in Seattle. The book's not only useful; it's a good read. Available through PlantAmnesty.

GROWING CALIFORNIA NATIVE PLANTS,
Marjorie Schmidt, University of California Press

A classic intro to native-plant cultivation and appreciation. Handy tables of plants for every situation—sun, shade, wet, dry—in the appendix.
Good for beginners, still good for experts.

NATIVE PLANTS FOR USE IN THE CALIFORNIA LANDSCAPE
Emile Labadie, Sierra City Press

Good companion volume for Schmidt, covering a select group of the most locally successful plants. The author founded Merritt College's Landscape Horticulture Department, and his work still anchors the native-plant hill there.

GARDENING FOR LOVE: THE MARKET BULLETINS
Elizabeth Lawrence, Duke University Press

GARDENING FROM THE HEART: WHY GARDENERS GARDEN
Carol Olwell, Antelope Island Press

Two very different books about the infinite variety of garden obsessions. Inspiring or monitory: you decide.

WHERE ON EARTH: A GUIDE TO SPECIALTY NURSERIES AND OTHER RESOURCES FOR CALIFORNIA GARDENERS
Barbara Stevens and Nancy Conner, Heyday Books

Picks up where this volume leaves off, strictly on the subject of nurseries. Not all nurseries in *Where on Earth* are retail sellers, and they're all over California. Feed your obsession! Sales benefit Golden Gate Park.

HORTUS THIRD
Staff of the L. H. Bailey Hortatorium, Cornell University, MacMillan

The other bible. If you know its Latin name, you can find almost any cultivated plant here, with its hometown and hints on how to treat it.

CALIFORNIA'S CHANGING LANDSCAPES: DIVERSITY AND CONSERVATION OF CALIFORNIA VEGETATION
Michael Barbour, Bruce Pavlik, Frank Drysdale, and Susan Lindstrom, California Native Plant Society

The prose (though marred by a small rash of typos, an epidemic lately) is a delight, more flowing and unified than the number of authors would lead one to expect, with a witty cultural-scientific reach, evident understanding, clarity, and a sense of process; it reads like elegantly compressed John McPhee. The book details what's around us, how it works and meshes, what has happened and is happening to it, and what may lie ahead. Since a great many of our garden plants, as well as pollinators and other inhabitants, originate in the natural systems around us, it's worth the gardener's attention.

Garden Style and/or Color in Your Garden
Penelope Hobhouse, Little, Brown

These remain favorites when I need a little inspiration. Coffee-table books with lots of color photographs and a sprinkle of good opinions. I cruise the remainder tables for this sort of thing.

While you're salivating over that glossy spread of a glorious border or of a five-course vegetarian meal in a magazine or coffee-table book, analyze it. Decide what you like about it. Is it the forms of the star plants? The contrast between foliage densities? Flower and leaf color? Nutrition? Season? (If you travel in July, you'll want later-season tomatoes, for example.) Density? Privacy, real or perceived? Focus on the plants (or other items) that give it those qualities; learn their names; then read up on them to see how they'll perform locally. Look in native-plant books and nurseries for plants that have what you want and will do well. Allow space for surprises.

Most important, read your land. Watch and see how long that patch is really in full sun, and find out how your books define it. Pick up a handful of soil and squeeze it. Just sit down and see what flies through. Look for deer and raccoon and 'possum tracks. Listen. You may come up with better ideas than the books.

One more trick: when everything's in and growing and showing off, if your garden still doesn't look as good as the pictures, take a photograph or two and look at those. You might be surprised. Maybe it's the frame or the focus; maybe it's just the glossy finish, but there's something about a picture that changes a garden from a worksite to a work of art.

FINDING BOOKS

We can find inspiration in the good bookstores, including used-book stores, that sprout all over the Bay Area; the fast way to find garden books is to walk into a store and scan around for a section where most of the books have green spines; it's like looking for the water in a dry field.

Bell's Books, at 536 Emerson Street in Palo Alto, is justly famous for garden and natural history books; so are Black Oak, on Shattuck Avenue in north Berkeley, and Green Apple, on Clement in San Francisco. At Green Apple you'll find all sorts of odd things (including minor jokes like *I Know Why the Caged Bird Sings* on the ornithology shelf). I like Graywolf Books, formerly Roskie and Wallace, on East 14th Street in San Leandro. Since its mild remodeling, I miss the Hudson automobile fenders hung at random, but appreciate being able to see the titles without a miner's headlamp. It's still good for 1949 forestry annuals, self-sufficiency gardening books from prehippie days, and the like—just the place to discover underappreciated garden writers of the last several decades.

Friends of the Library—any library—sales are good hunting spots for unexpected wonders and classics, too; that's where I got my copy of L. H. Bailey's GARDENER'S HANDBOOK for a mere fifty cents.

The problem with many of those inspiring garden books is that they have to be translated from the English. Specifically, from the British.

The British style of gardening was imported wholesale way back in colonial times, and with good reason. The northeastern colonists themselves were of course British in the majority, and gardened for food, medicines, decor, and other necessities the only way they knew. They brought their methods along with their seeds and, with a few famous and disastrous exceptions, both worked well. The soils and rainfall patterns of the eastern United States are similar enough to those of Britain and northern Eurasia; what the newcomers had to learn to take into account was the often much colder winters that the Gulf Stream spares similar latitudes in the old country. Obviously this made an impression. To this day, the first qualification you'll see in most plant catalogs is hardiness, which in Gardenese describes only a plant's resistance to freezing. A lot of hardy alpine rock garden species demonstrate that hardy doesn't mean anything like "tough" or "not particular" by being amazingly demanding and delicate in their own peculiar ways.

The British gardening tradition has enough to recommend it on its own merits. I like its exuberance, its adaptability, the way it honors the natural forms of plants and other materials, and its easy combination of practical and ornamental uses. Possibly more important to readers than these, or even than the lush and lovely way their gardens photograph, is the preeminence of the British in the field of garden writing. Such names as Vita Sackville-West and Gertrude Jekyll come to mind. Probably there are class aspirations and pretension at play here, too; professional gardeners joke that a British accent can double your income. The tendency of garden writers to come from or write for the upper classes seems to play right into our fantasies of building our own homegrown estates, at least until we're brought up short by something like Gertrude Jekyll's lead-in, "For those of you who have a moat . . . ."

Moat or no moat, one thing British gardeners of all classes can count on is rain. These folks invented the Wellington boot and the mackintosh coat for a reason. Most of eastern North America isn't quite so soggy, but gardeners there still get summer showers and can get away with Britified planting. In Northern California, we have to acknowledge that an expanse of lawn is as exotic a luxury as an acre of orchids. There are things a turf lawn does that nothing else does so well, but it's not the frame, the backdrop, the plain green wrapper that it is in the mysterious East. So there's one borrowed perception we need to turn inside-out.

Another mistaken borrowing concerns soil. Because of all that rain and its attendant conditions, eastern soils tend to be acidic, so eastern gardeners are forever buying lime and liming their soil. Out here, forget it. With rare exceptions, our soils are neutral to somewhat alkaline. Good old gypsum is a decent neutralizer (it neutralizes sodium, too, if you're in a hardpan-prone area), but organic matter—humus, compost, manure—will acidify and also fertilize, and is put to better use in the garden than in the dump. Use some to mulch rhodies, azaleas, camellias, and the other acid-lovers that keep turning sickly yellow between the veins, and they'll need less iron supplement.

Choosing plants like those, which are native to wet forests, is another piece of easternism. So is the fad for hostas, locally known as "snail chow." The rose fetish might be French, or British, or North American, or just good marketing, but I suspect part if it is that roses are plant hypochondriacs: always coming down with some alarming ugly disease, never quite dying. Rose gardeners can fuss endlessly with soil amendments, weird spray concoctions, pruning time and method, and novel theories of all sorts, and since you can't kill the damned things with a steamroller, they can all be right. A collection of books on roses closely resembles about a two centuries' span of books of child-care advice, and should make the reader similarly skeptical of experts.

Spring and planting go together in some parts of the world, but for a lot of plants (especially but not only natives), the best planting time here is fall. Certainly it's the best time for perennials to get their roots established, and local nurseries with their wits about them have a good stock of youngsters on hand, but they're bucking the national trend.

So we have to take all those easterners with a grain of salt. It's a good idea to look for a book's place of origin, as well as a plant's, and compensate accordingly.

INDEX

I

J

K

L

M